THE DEFINITIVE GUIDE TO DEFENCE AND STRATEGIC STUDIES

150 Q&A FOR MASTERY

THE VIYUG

To all the students who are pursuing degrees in defence and strategic studies, this book is dedicated to you. Your passion for learning and your commitment to serving our country is truly inspiring.

I also dedicate this book to all the teachers, mentors, and professors who have dedicated their lives to teaching and shaping the minds of the next generation of defence and strategic studies professionals. Your guidance and wisdom have been invaluable, and your impact on your students is immeasurable.

Finally, I would like to dedicate this book to my family and best friends, whose love and support has been unwavering throughout this journey. Your encouragement and belief in me have been the driving force behind this book, and I am grateful for everything that you have done for me.

Contents

"The art of war is simple enough. Find out where your enemy is. Get him as soon as you can. Strike him as hard as you can, and keep moving on."

- ULYSSES S. GRANT

Preface

Defence and Strategic Studies are becoming increasingly important in today's world. It is a complex field that requires a deep understanding of military strategy, national security, international relations and similar fields. The aim of this book is to provide students enrolled in this degree with a comprehensive guide to the subject matter.

This book contains 150 questions and answers that cover a wide range of topics related to defence and strategic studies. The questions are designed to challenge the reader's knowledge and understanding of the subject while providing valuable insights and perspectives. The answers are detailed and provide a thorough explanation of the concepts and theories covered in each question. Thus, the book is designed to be used as a study aid, helping students to prepare for exams. However, it can also be used as a reference guide for anyone interested in the field of defence and strategic studies.

It is important to note that this book is not intended to be a substitute for a complete course of study or professional advice. Rather, it is intended to be a study aid that complements a complete course of study. The reader should use their own judgement and consult with relevant experts as needed. I hope that you find this book to be a useful study aid and reference guide. With the hope that this book will be of great help to the students, on behalf of The Viyug, I wish great success to our readers.

Anirudh.R.Phadke

Acknowledgements

I would like to express my deepest gratitude to everyone who contributed to the creation of this book.

First and foremost, I would like to thank the students and professors of defence and strategic studies who have inspired me to write this book. Your passion for learning and your dedication to serving our country is truly admirable, and it is an honour to be able to contribute to your education.

I would also like to thank my friends and colleagues in the field of defence and strategic studies for their invaluable insights and contributions to this book. Your expertise and guidance have been instrumental in shaping this work.

I would like to thank my editing team for their support and assitance throughtout the publication process. Your dedication to producing high-quality works is truly remarkable.

Finally, I would like to express my deepest appreciation to my family and loved ones for their unwavering support and encouragement. Your belief in me has been a constant source of inspiration, and I am grateful for everything that you have done for me.

Thank you all for your contributions to this book. Your efforts have been invaluable, and I am deeply grateful for your support.

Anirudh.R.Phadke

Introduction

Defence and Strategic Studies are essential fields in today's world, with the security and stability of nations depending on a deep understanding of the intricacies of defence and strategic planning. As such, students enrolled in degree programmes in these fields need a comprehensive and detailed guide to help them navigate this complex subject matter.

This book, "The Definitive Guide to Defence and Strategic Studies: 150 Q&A for Mastery," is designed to provide just that. It is a comprehensive guide that covers a wide range of topics related to defence and strategic studies, including the history of warfare, military strategy, international relations, and much more.

The book is organised into 150 questions and answers, each designed to challenge the reader's knowledge and understanding of the subject matter. The questions cover both basic and advanced concepts, making it suitable for students at all levels of study. Additionally, each answer is accompanied by a detailed explanation, providing the reader with a thorough understanding of the topic at hand.

As you work your way through this book, you will gain a deeper appreciation for the complexities of defence and strategic studies. You will learn about the different types of warfare, from conventional to unconventional, and the strategies and tactics used to combat them. You will also gain an understanding of the geopolitical and historical contexts that have shaped our world, and the role that defence and strategic planning plays in maintaining stability and security.

Whether you are a student enrolled in a defence and strategic studies programme or simply someone interested in the field, this book will serve as an invaluable resource. It will challenge your understanding of the subject matter and deepen your knowledge, providing you with a comprehensive and detailed guide to defence and strategic studies.

CHAPTER ONE

QUESTIONS CATALOGUE

List of all Q&A in this book

1. Explain the scope of the degree in 'Defence and Strategic Studies'?
2. Explain the concept of national security?
3. What is the role of defence in national security?
4. What is the significance of strategic studies in modern warfare?
5. State the differences between strategy and tactics?
6. Explain the role of intelligence in national security?
7. Explain the concept of nuclear deterrence?
8. Explain the role of diplomacy in national security?
9. What is the significance of military alliances in international security?
10. What is the relationship between military strategy and political strategy?
11. Explain the impact of technological advances on modern warfare?
12. What role do non-state actors play in modern warfare?
13. Define the concept of asymmetric warfare.
14. Explain the relationship between terrorism and national security?
15. What is the impact of globalisation on national security?
16. What is the importance of economic security in national security?
17. State the role of the military in disaster management?
18. Define the concept of cybersecurity.
19. State the significance of space security in national security?
20. Explain the role of intelligence agencies in counterterrorism operations?
21. State the impact of climate change on national security?
22. Define the concept of human security.
23. What is the relationship between democracy and national security?

24. Explain the role of media in national security?
25. Define the impact of propaganda on national security?
26. Define the concept of hybrid warfare?
27. Explain the role of Private Military Companies (PMCs) in modern warfare?
28. State the impact of globalisation on military strategy?
29. What is the relationship between nationalism and national security?
30. How do ethnic and religious conflicts affect national security?
31. How do international organisations contribute to the maintenance of global security? *OR* How does the United Nations contribute to the maintenance of international security?
32. Define the concept of deterrence in international relations.
33. How do military doctrines influence defence policy development?
34. How does military spending affect national security?
35. Why is maritime security important to national security?
36. Define the concept of military strategy.
37. How do arms control treaties contribute to the prevention of nuclear weapons proliferation?
38. How do cyber attacks affect national security?
39. Define the concept of war termination.
40. How does strategic culture influence the development of national security policy?
41. How are intelligence and military operations interconnected? *OR* What is the relationship between intelligence and military operations?
42. How does terrorism affect the relationship between civilians and the military?
43. What is the role of military education in developing strategic thinkers?
44. What is the importance of defence industry in national security?
45. Define the concept of unconventional warfare.
46. What is the impact of modern information technologies on military operations?
47. How does military intelligence contribute to the decision making process?
48. How does historical analysis contribute to the understanding of military strategy?
49. Define the concept of pre-emption in national security.
50. How does military technology influence the dynamics of the battlefield?

51. How significant is strategic communication in the context of national security?
52. Define the concept of insurgency.
53. How do special operations forces contribute to modern warfare?
54. How do drone technologies affect military operations?
55. Why is the relationship between civilians and the military significant in democratic societies?
56. Define the concept of psychological warfare.
57. Briefly explain the use of gas warfare in the Second World War?
58. Briefly explain the concept of city-states?
59. Briefly explain the concept of indirect democracy?
60. Briefly explain the concept of lobbying?
61. How significant is the role of international law in controlling the application of force in the context of international relations?
62. What is the concept of Grey Zone conflicts and their impications for national security?
63. Briefly explain the role and powers of India's Chief of Defence Staff (CDS)?
64. Briefly explain the objectives of India's National Security Guard (NSG)?
65. Briefly explain the Higher Defence Organisation of China?
66. Breifly explain the Higher Defence Organisation of India?
67. What are the needs for defence production?
68. Briefly explain the merits and demerits of foreign sources in defence sector?
69. Explain in detail about Defence Planning in India since 1962?
70. What were the reasons for the partition of India and Pakistan?
71. Discuss the reasons for the refugee crisis in East Pakistan during 1970-71?
72. What were the major events of the 1962 Sino-Indian War?
73. Provide a chronological outline of the Kargil war of 1999 and how Indian military emerged successful despite various challenges.
74. What are the different ways in which Kashmir question continue to affect India even today?
75. What according to Treaty Provision forbids attack on uninhabited land?
76. What are the merits and demerits of codification of International Law?
77. Briefly explain the geostrategic location of Indian Ocean?
78. What is the concept of Fourth Generation Warfare and its implications for military strategy?

79. What is the impact of environmental degradation on national security?
80. What is the concept of network-centric warfare and its implications for military operations?
81. What is the role of unmanned systems in modern warfare?
82. How has the concept of deterrence evolved since the end of Cold War?
83. What is the impact of global pandemics on national security?
84. Define the concept of "grey swans" in national security.
85. Define the concept of "lethal autonomy" in military technology.
86. Define the concept of "deep fakes" in information warfare.
87. What is the impact of commercialisation of space on national security?
88. What is the impact of water security on regional security?
89. Define the concept of "bunker busters" in military technology.
90. What is the concept of "just war theory" and its relevance to modern warfare?
91. Define the concept of "Greymail."
92. What is the impact of political polarisation on military operations?
93. What is the impact of the Fourth Industrial Revolution on military operations?
94. What is the impact of the COVID-19 pandemic on military readiness and operations?
95. What is the concept of "fifth-generation warfare" and its implications for national security?
96. What is the concept of "dark data" and its implications for military intelligence analysis?
97. What is the impact of rise of autocratic regimes on global security?
98. Define the concept of "strategic empathy" in military diplomacy.
99. Define the concept of "strategic foresight" and its implications for military planning.
100. Explain the concept of "algorithmic warfare" and its implications for national security?
101. Explain the concept of "biodefence" and its relevance to national security?
102. Explain the impact of the rise of populism on global security?
103. How can the military contribute to the promotion of sustainable energy management in regions affected by conflict?
104. How does the increase in authoritarianism affect global security and democracy?

105. Explain the Gandhian approach and its relevance today in conflict resolution?

106. Examine the initiatives and effectivness of CBMs between India and Pakistan?

107. Discuss various challenges to India's foreign policy in South Asia?

108. What is the significance of great game in Afghanistan?

109. Describe the different political systems followed by the South Asian countries?

110. What are the key highlights in India-Maldives relationship?

111. Explain the non-traditional security threats confronting India-Bangladesh relationship?

112. Is Military - Media relationship complimentary or conflictual? Discuss.

113. How the brain-mapping technology can be used for military operations?

114. Write about the scope of Peace and Conflict Studies?

115. Explain the Communist approach to war?

116. Do you think that Indian Armed Forces are capable of facing its adversaries? Critically analyse.

117. Is the use of nuclear weapons ever justified in modern warfare?

118. Should military spending be decreased to allocate more funds for social welfare programmes?

119. To what extent should autonomous weapons be allowed in military operations?

120. Should countries to be allowed to acquire and maintain their own nuclear arsenals?

121. Should there be limits on the use of drone strikes in counter-terrorism operations?

122. Is it appropriate for military organisations to collaborate with private intelligence firms?

123. Should private companies be allowed to develop and sell military weapons and technology?

124. Should the use of chemical and biological weapons be considered a red line in international conflicts?

125. Is pre-emptive military action ever justified to prevent the proliferation of weapons of mass destruction?

126. Is it ethical for governments to use propaganda and psychological operations in warfare?

127. Is it necessary to priortise non-military approaches, such as economic aid and diplomacy, over military solutions to resolve conflicts?

128. Should countries be held accountable for the use of military force against non-state actors operating within their borders?

129. Should military be involved in domestic law enforcement and border security?

130. Can the use of torture be justified in the interrogation of suspected terrorists?

131. Should countries have a moral duty to intervene in cases of genocide and mass atrocities, even if it requires violating national sovereignty?

132. Should there be a global ban on the use of landmines and cluster munitions in warfare?

133. Should countries be allowed to engage in cyber espionage and sabotage against their economic rivals?

134. How can the military balance the need for operational security with the need for transparency and accountability to the public?

135. What role does leadership play in shaping the success or failure of military campaigns and operations?

136. What are the challenges faced by the military in implementing its doctrines and strategies in modern warfare scenarios?

137. How can military alliances and partnerships effectively address global security challenges, particularly in the context of shifting geopolitical dynamics?

138. What are the ethical implications of using military force and how can they be effectively addressed in decision-making processes?

139. How can the military effectively engage with local communities and stakeholders in conflict-affected regions, and what role can civil-military relations play in achieving long-term stability and peace?

140. What is the future of nuclear deterrence and disarmament, particularly in the context of increasing proliferation risks and the emergence of new nuclear powers?

141. Should countries pursue territorial expansion in pursuit of national security?

142. To what extent should civilians be involved in military decision-making processes?

143. What is the role of gender in military operations and how can it be better integrated into military planning?

144. How can militaries better incorporate emerging technologies, such as artifical intelligence and quantum computing, into their operations?

145. How can militaries balance the need for secrecy and security with the public's right to information and transparency?

146. Is the current global arms trade ethical, and what measures can be taken to regulate it more effectively?

147. Is there a need for a global ban on the development and use of killer robots, and what are the potential implications of their use in warfare?

148. Is the practice of targeted killings morally justifiable in the context of counterterrorism?

149. Should soldiers be held accountable for war crimes committed during conflict, even if they were following orders?

150. How has India's defence modernisation programme evolved over the years, and what are the major priorities for the Indian Armed Forces in the coming years?

CHAPTER TWO

150 QUESTIONS AND ANSWERS

Disclaimer: While "The Definitive Guide to Defence and Strategic Studies: 150 Q&A for Mastery" has been written to provide accurate and up-to-date information, the author and publisher are not responsible for any errors or omissions or for any consequences arising from the use of the information contained in this book. The book is intended solely as a study aid and should not be used as a substitute for a complete course of study or professional advice. Readers should use their own judgement and consult with relevant experts as needed. The author and publisher do not guarantee the accuracy, completeness, or timeliness of the information presented in this book.

1. Explain the scope of the degree in 'Defence and Strategic Studies'?

A degree in defence and strategic studies is an academic program that focuses on the study of national security, defence policy, military strategy, and other related fields. It provides students with a comprehensive understanding of the factors that contribute to the security and stability of nations, as well as the skills necessary to develop and implement effective defence strategies. The curriculum of a degree in defence and strategic studies typically includes courses on topics such as military history, national security policy, defence technology, conflict resolution, and international relations. Students are also trained in critical thinking, research, and analysis, which are essential skills for those pursuing careers in the military, government, or the private sector.

Graduates of a defence and strategic studies degree can pursue a variety of careers, including military service, defence contracting, intelligence analysis, diplomacy, and public policy. They may also go on to pursue further education in fields such as law, international relations, or business. The importance of defence and strategic studies has only increased in recent years, with global instability and the threat of terrorism posing significant challenges to national security. As such, this degree program is an excellent option for students interested in pursuing a career in a field that is both intellectually stimulating and socially relevant.

2. Explain the concept of national security?

National security refers to the protection and preservation of a nation's people, territory, and interests against threats and dangers, both internal and external. It encompasses a range of issues and concerns, including military defence, intelligence gathering, law enforcement, economic stability, and diplomacy. The concept of national security is a complex and multifaceted one, as it involves balancing the need for protection and security with the need to maintain individual rights and freedoms. In addition, what is considered a threat to national security can vary depending on the nation, its geopolitical context, and its historical and cultural factors.

Some common threats to national security include terrorism, cyberattacks, military aggression, economic instability, and natural disasters. To address these threats, governments may employ a variety of strategies, including military action, intelligence gathering, diplomatic negotiations, economic sanctions, and the implementation of security policies and procedures. National security is a critical aspect of governance, as it plays a vital role in ensuring the safety and well-being of a nation's citizens. However, achieving effective national security requires a careful balance between security and liberty, as well as a deep understanding of the various factors that contribute to national security threats.

3. What is the role of defence in national security?

Defence is a critical component of national security, as it is responsible for protecting a nation's borders, people, and interests against external threats. The primary role of defence in national security is to provide a military capability that can deter aggression and respond effectively to any security threats that may arise. A well-functioning defence system is essential to maintain the sovereignty of a nation and protect it from external threats. The defence sector is responsible for developing and implementing military strategies, acquiring, and maintaining weapons systems, and training and deploying personnel to respond to potential security challenges.

In addition to its traditional role in protecting against military aggression, defence also plays a crucial role in responding to non-traditional security threats such as cyberattacks, terrorism, and natural disasters. Defence agencies work closely with other branches of government, including law enforcement and intelligence agencies, to identify and respond to these emerging threats. In summary, the role of defence in national security is to provide a military capability that can deter aggression and respond effectively to any security threats that may arise. A strong and effective defence system is essential for maintaining national sovereignty and protecting the people and interests of a nation.

4. What is the significance of strategic studies in modern warfare?

Strategic studies are important in modern warfare as they provide critical insights into the planning and execution of military operations. The modern battlefield is complex and dynamic, with numerous variables that can affect the outcome of a conflict. Strategic studies provide a framework for understanding these variables, enabling military planners and commanders to make informed decisions that maximise the chances of success.

One of the key contributions of strategic studies is the development of military strategies and doctrines that consider the unique characteristics of modern warfare. This includes the use of advanced technologies such as drones, cyber warfare, and artificial intelligence, as well as the integration of traditional military capabilities such as infantry and artillery. Another important contribution of strategic studies is the development of methods for analysing and interpreting military intelligence. This includes the use of advanced data analysis techniques, as well as the development of models and simulations that can help predict the outcomes of military operations.

Finally, strategic studies play a critical role in shaping the broader policy context in which modern warfare takes place. This includes issues such as arms control, disarmament, and international cooperation on security matters. By providing a framework for understanding the complex and interrelated factors that contribute to modern warfare, strategic studies help policymakers develop effective strategies for promoting peace and security. In summary, strategic studies are essential in modern warfare as they provide critical insights into the planning and execution of military operations, help develop military strategies and doctrines, enable military intelligence analysis, and shape broader policy contexts for promoting peace and security.

5. State the differences between strategy and tactics?

Strategy	Tactics
Long term planning and decision-making process	Short-term planning and decision-making process
Focuses on achieving broader objectives and goals	Focuses on achieving specific objectives and goals
Concerned with allocating resources and determining the best approach for achieving a goal	Concerned with executing specific actions to achieve a goal
Involves high-level decision-makers such as executives, commanders, or policymakers	Involves lower-level decision makers such as managers, supervisors, or frontline personnel
Tends to be more flexible and adaptable to changing circumstances	Tends to be more rigid and structured
Considers the broader context, including environmental, social, and political factors	Focuses on the immediate context, including tactical challenges and opportunities
Involves multiple tactics working in concert to achieve a strategic objective	Involves individual tactics executed in sequence or in parallel

In summary, strategy is a long-term planning and decision-making process that focuses on achieving broader objectives and goals, while tactics are a short-term planning and decision-making process that focuses on achieving specific objectives and goals. Strategy involves high-level decision-makers and considers the broader context, while tactics involve lower-level decision-makers and focus on the immediate context. Strategy tends to be more flexible and adaptable, while tactics tend to be more rigid and structured. Both strategy and tactics are essential for achieving success in any endeavour, including military operations, business, and sports.

6. Explain the role of intelligence in national security?

Intelligence plays a critical role in national security by providing policymakers and military leaders with timely and accurate information about potential security threats. The role of intelligence is to gather, analyse, and disseminate information that can help inform decisions on matters related to national security. One of the key roles of intelligence is to identify and assess potential security threats, both domestic and international. This includes monitoring activities of foreign governments and organisations, tracking the movements of terrorist groups, and identifying emerging threats such as cyber-attacks and biological warfare. By providing early warning of potential threats, intelligence agencies enable policymakers and military leaders to take pre-emptive action to mitigate risks and protect national interests.

Another critical role of intelligence is to support military operations by providing real-time intelligence on the battlefield. This includes monitoring enemy movements, identifying targets, and providing situational awareness to commanders in the field. By providing accurate and timely intelligence, military leaders can make informed decisions that increase the chances of mission success and minimise the risk of casualties. Intelligence also plays a key role in supporting law enforcement efforts to maintain domestic security. This includes monitoring criminal activities, identifying threats to public safety, and providing evidence to support criminal prosecutions. Intelligence agencies work closely with law enforcement agencies to identify and disrupt criminal networks and prevent terrorist attacks.

In summary, intelligence plays a critical role in national security by providing policymakers and military leaders with timely and accurate information about potential security threats. The role of intelligence is to gather, analyse, and disseminate information that can help inform decisions on matters related to national security, support military operations, and maintain domestic security. Intelligence is essential for ensuring the safety and security of a nation and its people.

7. Explain the concept of nuclear deterrence?

Nuclear deterrence is a concept in international relations that aims to prevent a nuclear war by maintaining a credible threat of retaliation. The basic idea of nuclear deterrence is that if a state possesses nuclear weapons, and the other states believe that the state will use them in response to any nuclear attack, then the other states will be deterred from launching an attack in the first place. The logic of nuclear deterrence assumes that no state would want to engage in a conflict that would result in mutual destruction. Therefore, the possession of nuclear weapons creates a situation where the cost of launching a nuclear attack would be higher than any potential gain. This is why nuclear deterrence is considered a stable strategy for maintaining peace between nuclear-armed states.

The effectiveness of nuclear deterrence depends on several factors, including the perceived credibility of a state's nuclear arsenal, the state's willingness to use nuclear weapons, and the nature of the potential threat. Nuclear deterrence has been a key component of international security since the Cold War, with many countries investing heavily in nuclear weapons and delivery systems to maintain their deterrent posture.

However, the concept of nuclear deterrence is not without its critics, who argue that the potential consequences of a nuclear war are too catastrophic to justify relying on deterrence as a strategy. Some experts also worry about the risk of accidental nuclear war, where a misunderstanding or technical malfunction could trigger a nuclear exchange. Despite these concerns, nuclear deterrence remains a central concept in international relations and is likely to continue to shape global security dynamics for the foreseeable future.

8. Explain the role of diplomacy in national security?

Diplomacy plays a crucial role in national security by enabling countries to achieve their security objectives through peaceful means, such as negotiations and dialogue. Diplomatic efforts can prevent or mitigate conflicts, reduce tensions, and foster cooperation between countries. Diplomacy can also help to promote economic and political stability, which are critical factors in ensuring national security. One of the primary roles of diplomacy in national security is to prevent conflicts and manage crises. Diplomatic efforts can help to reduce tensions between countries and resolve disputes before they escalate into military conflict. Diplomats can work to identify common interests and negotiate agreements that can help to prevent or mitigate potential threats.

Diplomacy also plays a key role in promoting international cooperation on issues such as counterterrorism, non-proliferation, and cybersecurity. Diplomats can work together to develop shared strategies and initiatives to address common threats, such as international terrorism, and prevent the spread of weapons of mass destruction.

Another critical role of diplomacy in national security is to promote economic and political stability. Diplomats can work to promote economic development, improve governance, and strengthen democratic institutions in other countries. These efforts can help to reduce the likelihood of conflict, promote regional stability, and create more opportunities for economic growth and prosperity. In summary, diplomacy is a critical component of national security, as it can help to prevent conflicts, manage crises, and promote cooperation between countries. Diplomats can work to identify common interests, negotiate agreements, and promote economic and political stability. By using diplomacy to achieve their security objectives, countries can avoid the costs and risks associated with military conflict and build a more stable and secure world.

9. What is the significance of military alliances in international security?

Military alliances are an essential component of international security, as they enable countries to pool their resources, coordinate their defence efforts, and deter potential adversaries. Military alliances can help to enhance the security of member countries by increasing their military capabilities, providing a framework for joint military operations, and promoting greater cooperation between countries.

One of the primary benefits of military alliances is deterrence. By banding together in a military alliance, countries can send a strong message to potential adversaries that any attack on one member state will be met with a coordinated response from the entire alliance. This can help to deter potential aggressors and prevent conflicts from escalating. Military alliances can also help to enhance the military capabilities of member states. By working together, countries can pool their resources, share intelligence, and coordinate their defence efforts, making it possible to undertake joint military operations that would be beyond the capacity of individual countries. Another benefit of military alliances is the promotion of greater cooperation and trust between member countries. By working together in a military alliance, countries can build relationships, share knowledge and expertise, and develop greater trust and confidence in one another. This can help to reduce tensions between countries and promote regional stability and security.

Military alliances are also important for promoting global stability and security. By providing a framework for coordinated military action, military alliances can help to prevent conflicts from spreading beyond their region of origin and contribute to the maintenance of international peace and security. In summary, military alliances play a crucial role in international security by enhancing deterrence, promoting greater military capabilities and cooperation, building trust and confidence between countries, and contributing to global stability and security.

10. What is the relationship between military strategy and political strategy?

Military strategy and political strategy are closely related, as military actions are often guided by political objectives, and military operations can have significant political consequences. Political strategy is concerned with the overall goals and objectives of a country's foreign and domestic policies. It involves a range of activities, such as diplomatic negotiations, economic sanctions, and political pressure, aimed at achieving a country's political objectives. Military strategy, on the other hand, is concerned with the use of military force to achieve a country's military objectives, such as defeating an enemy or protecting a country's territorial integrity.

Military strategy and political strategy are interconnected because military operations can have significant political consequences. The use of military force can help to achieve political objectives, such as changing the behaviour of an adversary, enforcing compliance with international norms, or deterring potential adversaries from taking aggressive action. However, military operations can also have negative political consequences if they are not aligned with a country's broader political objectives. Military actions that are not guided by a clear political strategy can lead to unintended consequences, such as civilian casualties, damage to infrastructure, and the destabilisation of a region.

Therefore, it is essential to ensure that military strategy is aligned with political objectives and that military actions are carefully planned and executed to achieve those objectives. Military planners must work closely with political leaders to ensure that military operations are consistent with broader political goals and that the use of military force is justified and appropriate given the political context.

11. Explain the impact of technological advances on modern warfare?

Technological advances have had a significant impact on modern warfare, changing the way wars are fought, and the strategies employed by militaries. The following are some of the keyways in which technological advances have impacted modern warfare;

1. <u>Precision Targeting</u>: Advances in technology have made it possible to conduct precision targeting of military assets, such as vehicles, aircrafts, and weapons systems. This has made it easier to destroy enemy targets while minimising civilian casualties and collateral damage.
2. <u>Increased situational awareness</u>: Technological advances have also enabled militaries to have a better understanding of the battlefield, including the location of enemy forces, terrain, and weather conditions. This has allowed for more effective planning and execution of military operations.
3. <u>Improved communication</u>: Advances in communication technology have enabled militaries to communicate more effectively and efficiently with each other, reducing the likelihood of miscommunication and improving coordination.
4. <u>Autonomous weapons systems</u>: The development of autonomous weapons systems, such as drones, has changed the way wars are fought, allowing for more precise targeting, and reducing the risk of casualties among military personnel.
5. <u>Cyber warfare</u>: Technological advances have also led to emergence of cyber warfare, where militaries use technology to attack enemy computer systems, disrupt communications, and gain a strategic advantage.

Overall, technological advances have had a significant impact on modern warfare, changing the way wars are fought, and the strategies employed by militaries. These advances have made it possible to conduct military operations with greater precision, efficiency, and effectiveness, but they have also raised ethical concerns and highlighted the importance of responsible use of technology in warfare.

12. What role do non-state actors play in modern warfare?

Non-state actors, such as insurgent groups, terrorist organisations, and private military companies, play an increasingly important role in modern warfare. The following are some of the keyways in which non-state actors impact modern warfare;

1. <u>Asymmetric warfare</u>: Non-state actors often lack the resources and capabilities of state actors, so they rely on asymmetric tactics, such as guerrilla warfare, sabotage, and terrorism, to achieve their objectives. This can make them difficult to defeat, as they are not bound by the same rules of engagement and may operate in areas where conventional military operations are difficult.
2. <u>Cyber warfare</u>: Non-state actors can also engage in cyber warfare, using technology to disrupt communication networks, steal sensitive information, and launch attacks on critical infrastructure.
3. <u>Proxy warfare</u>: Non-state actors can serve as proxies for larger states, either by receiving funding, training, or equipment from state actors, or by operating on their behalf in a conflict zone.
4. <u>Humanitarian aid</u>: Non-state actors can also play a role in providing humanitarian aid and assistance to civilian populations affected by conflict, particularly in areas where state actors are unable or unwilling to provide such support.

Overall, non-state actors play an important and complex role in modern warfare. They can pose significant challenges to state actors, but they can also provide valuable support and assistance in conflict zones. As the nature of warfare continues to evolve, it is likely that the role of non-state actors will continue to grow in importance.

13. Define the concept of asymmetric warfare.

Asymmetric warfare is a type of conflict where one side has a significant military advantage over the other, leading the weaker side to rely on unconventional tactics to achieve their objectives. Asymmetric warfare is typically characterised by the following:

1. <u>Insurgency</u>: Insurgents use unconventional tactics, such as guerrilla warfare, sabotage, and terrorism, to disrupt the operations of the stronger military force and achieve their objectives.
2. <u>Improvised weaponry</u>: Asymmetric warfare often involves the use of improvised weapons, such as homemade explosives, which can be highly effective against conventional military forces.
3. <u>Cyber warfare</u>: Asymmetric warfare can also involve the use of cyber-attacks to disrupt communication networks, steal sensitive information, and launch attacks on critical infrastructure.
4. <u>Strategic communications</u>: Asymmetric warfare may also involve the use of strategic communications to shape public opinion and influence the perception of the conflict.

Asymmetric warfare presents significant challenges to conventional military forces, as it requires them to adapt to unconventional tactics and operate in complex and often hostile environments. The effectiveness of asymmetric tactics can depend on several factors, including the strength of the conventional military force, the political climate, and the level of public support for the conflict. Asymmetric warfare is becoming increasingly common in modern conflicts, as non-state actors and other unconventional forces seek to challenge conventional military power.

14. Explain the relationship between terrorism and national security?

Terrorism poses a significant threat to national security, as it can cause widespread fear and disruption, destabilise governments, and undermine the rule of law. The relationship between terrorism and national security can be understood in the following ways:

1. <u>Threat to civilians</u>: Terrorism is primarily directed against civilian populations and can result in significant loss of life and injury. This creates a sense of fear and insecurity in the population, which can undermine the stability of the government and its ability to maintain law and order.

2. <u>Economic impact</u>: Terrorism can also have a significant economic impact, by disrupting critical infrastructure, reducing tourism and foreign investment, and increasing the cost of security measures.
3. <u>Political instability</u>: Terrorism can also lead to political instability, by creating divisions within society and among political leaders, and by challenging the legitimacy of the government and its ability to protect its citizens.
4. <u>International relations</u>: Terrorism can also impact international relations, by creating tensions between nations and by affecting trade and diplomatic relations.

In response to the threat of terrorism, many governments have developed strategies and policies aimed at enhancing national security. These may include increased security measures, intelligence gathering and analysis, and efforts to prevent the radicalisation of individuals and groups. The relationship between terrorism and national security is complex and multifaceted and requires a comprehensive approach that considers the political, social, economic, and technological factors that contribute to the threat of terrorism.

15. What is the impact of globalisation on national security?

Globalisation has had a significant impact on national security, both positive and negative. On the positive side, globalisation has increased international cooperation and reduced the likelihood of large-scale conflict between nations. It has also facilitated the exchange of information and ideas, making it easier for governments to monitor and respond to security threats. However, globalisation has also created new security challenges. One of the most significant is the increased ease with which terrorist organisations can operate globally. Globalisation has enabled these groups to recruit members, obtain funding, and plan attacks from virtually anywhere in the world. Additionally, it has made it easier for organised crime syndicates to operate across national borders, trafficking drugs, weapons, and people.

Furthermore, globalisation has led to the growth of multinational corporations, which have become major players in international affairs. While these companies can bring significant economic benefits to countries, they can also have a negative impact on national security. For example, they may be more loyal to their shareholders than to the countries in which they operate, and their actions could undermine national security interests. Overall, the impact of globalisation on national security is complex and multifaceted. It has both positive and negative effects, and it requires careful management and planning to ensure that countries can maintain their security in a rapidly changing world.

16. What is the importance of economic security in national security?

Economic security is a critical component of national security. A nation's economic strength directly impacts its ability to provide for the basic needs of its citizens, to fund its military and security apparatus, and to project power and influence globally. A strong economy provides a stable foundation for a nation's security, while a weak economy can undermine its ability to protect itself and its interests.

There are several ways in which economic security contributes to national security. First, a strong economy allows a country to invest in its military and security infrastructure, ensuring that it can defend itself against external threats. Second, economic security enables a country to provide for the basic needs of its citizens, such as food, shelter, and healthcare, reducing the likelihood of social unrest and instability. Third, economic security enables a country to project its influence globally, through trade and investment, diplomacy, and cultural exchange. However, economic security can also be a source of vulnerability. Economic dependence on other nations or regions can create risks for a country, as disruptions to the global economy can have cascading effects on national security. In addition, economic inequality and poverty can lead to social unrest and instability, which can threaten national security.

In summary, economic security is a critical component of national security. A strong economy enables a country to provide for the needs of its citizens, invest in its security infrastructure, and project its influence globally. However, economic dependence and inequality can also create risks for national security. Governments must therefore prioritise economic security as part of their broader national security strategies.

17. State the role of the military in disaster management?

The military plays a critical role in disaster management, particularly in responding to large-scale natural disasters or other emergencies that require a coordinated, rapid response. The military's unique capabilities, including its logistical expertise, advanced communications equipment, and specialised training, make it well-suited for disaster relief operations.

One of the primary roles of the military in disaster management is to provide logistical support. This includes transporting personnel, equipment, and supplies to the affected area, setting up temporary shelters and medical facilities, and providing transportation and support for relief workers and victims. The military's ability to quickly mobilise resources and personnel can be critical in the early stages of a disaster when time is of the essence. The military can also provide critical support for search and rescue operations. Military personnel are often trained in specialised search and rescue techniques, and their experience in challenging environments can be invaluable in disaster situations. In addition, military helicopters and other specialised equipment can be used to access hard-to-reach areas and transport victims to safety. Finally, the military can play a key role in providing security and maintaining order in the aftermath of a disaster. This can include securing the affected area, providing support for law enforcement and other emergency responders, and preventing looting and other criminal activities.

Overall, the military's role in disaster management is multifaceted and critical. Its unique capabilities and expertise can be invaluable in responding to large-scale emergencies and helping to save lives and provide critical support to those affected by disasters.

18. Define the concept of cybersecurity.

Cybersecurity refers to the practice of protecting computer systems, networks, and sensitive information from cyber threats such as hacking, malware, and data breaches. It encompasses a range of techniques, technologies, and best practices that are designed to prevent unauthorised access to computer systems and protect against damage or theft of data. Cybersecurity is essential in today's world, where virtually all aspects of our lives are dependent on technology and the internet. Cyber-attacks can cause significant damage to businesses, governments, and individuals, ranging from financial losses to reputational damage and even physical harm.

Effective cybersecurity involves a multi-layered approach that includes both technological and human elements. It includes implementing strong passwords and access controls, regularly updating software and security patches, using firewalls and other security technologies, and providing training and education to employees to help them recognise and avoid cyber threats.

Cybersecurity also involves a proactive approach to threat detection and response. This includes monitoring networks and systems for suspicious activity, using threat intelligence to identify and mitigate emerging threats, and having a plan in place to respond quickly and effectively in the event of a cyber-attack. Overall, cybersecurity is a critical component of modern society, and it requires ongoing attention and investment to ensure that computer systems and sensitive information remain secure and protected against the ever-evolving landscape of cyber threats.

19. State the significance of space security in national security?

Space security is becoming increasingly important in national security due to the growing dependence of modern militaries and economies on space-based technologies. Satellites are essential for communication, navigation, weather forecasting, and other critical functions, and disruptions to these systems could have significant implications for national security.

The importance of space security in national security can be seen in several key areas. First, space-based technologies are critical for military operations, including intelligence gathering, surveillance, and communication. Disruptions to these systems could undermine a nation's ability to defend itself and project power. Second, space-based technologies are also essential for civilian infrastructure and services, including transportation, emergency response, and finance. Disruptions to these systems could have significant economic and social consequences, potentially leading to disruptions in supply chains, financial markets, and other critical areas.

Finally, space security is also important from a global perspective, as the use of space-based technologies is becoming increasingly common among countries around the world. This has led to concerns about the militarisation of space and the potential for conflict in this arena. To address these concerns, nations are increasingly focused on developing space situational awareness capabilities, improving cybersecurity for space-based systems, and developing international norms and agreements to promote responsible behaviour in space. Overall, the importance of space security in national security is clear, and it will continue to be a critical area of focus for governments and militaries around the world.

20. Explain the role of intelligence agencies in counterterrorism operations?

Intelligence agencies play a critical role in counterterrorism operations by gathering and analysing information about potential terrorist threats and providing this information to law enforcement and military agencies. The role of intelligence agencies in counterterrorism operations can be broken down into three key areas: collection, analysis, and dissemination. First, intelligence agencies are responsible for collecting information about potential terrorist threats from a variety of sources, including human intelligence, signals intelligence, and open-source intelligence. This information may include details about the identities, intentions, and capabilities of terrorist groups, as well as information about specific plots or attacks.

Second, intelligence agencies analyse this information to identify potential threats and assess their likelihood and potential impact. This analysis may involve identifying patterns and trends in terrorist activities, as well as assessing the credibility and reliability of sources.

Finally, intelligence agencies disseminate this information to law enforcement and military agencies, as well as to policymakers and other stakeholders. This information may be used to inform law enforcement investigations, military operations, and other counterterrorism efforts. Overall, the role of intelligence agencies in counterterrorism operations is critical, as they provide the information and analysis needed to identify and neutralize potential threats before they can be carried out. Intelligence agencies work closely with law enforcement and military agencies to develop and implement effective strategies to combat terrorism, and their efforts are essential for maintaining national security and protecting citizens from terrorist attacks.

21. State the impact of climate change on national security?

Climate change is having a significant impact on national security, as it is contributing to a range of environmental and social challenges that can undermine the stability and security of nations around the world. Some of the key impacts of climate change on national security include:

1. <u>Resource scarcity</u>: Climate change can lead to water shortages, food insecurity, and other resource scarcities that can contribute to conflict and social instability.
2. <u>Displacement</u>: As climate change worsens, natural disasters and sea level rise are likely to displace large numbers of people, leading to increased migration and potential conflict.
3. <u>Infrastructure damage</u>: Climate change can damage critical infrastructure, such as transportation systems, energy grids, and military installations, compromising a nation's ability to defend itself and project power.
4. <u>Geopolitical shifts</u>: Climate change can alter geopolitical power dynamics, as nations with abundant natural resources and strategic locations become more valuable and influential.
5. <u>Global instability</u>: Climate change is likely to exacerbate existing political and social tensions, potentially leading to increased conflict and instability on a global scale.

To address these challenges, nations around the world are increasingly focused on developing strategies to mitigate the impacts of climate change and adapt to its effects. This includes investing in renewable energy and other climate-friendly technologies, developing infrastructure that is resilient to climate change, and working to address the root causes of climate change through international cooperation and collaboration. Overall, the impact of climate change on national security is significant and requires ongoing attention and investment to address effectively.

22. Define the concept of human security.

Human security is a concept that refers to the protection and well-being of individuals, communities, and societies from a range of threats and challenges, including poverty, disease, conflict, environmental degradation, and other forms of social and economic insecurity. The concept of human security emerged in the 1990s in response to a growing recognition that traditional security concepts, which focused primarily on military threats and interstate conflict, were inadequate for addressing the complex and interconnected challenges facing individuals and communities around the world.

Human security emphasises the importance of addressing the root causes of insecurity, including poverty, inequality, and social exclusion, and promoting the rights and dignity of all individuals. This includes a focus on protecting vulnerable groups, such as women, children, and marginalised communities, and ensuring that individuals have access to necessities such as food, water, and healthcare.

Human security is a broad and multidimensional concept that encompasses a range of social, economic, and political factors. It recognises that individuals and communities are interconnected and that addressing the needs and concerns of one group can have positive ripple effects throughout society. Overall, the concept of human security is an important framework for addressing the complex and interconnected challenges facing individuals and communities around the world, and it is increasingly being adopted by governments, civil society organisations, and international institutions as a guiding principle for policy and practice.

23. What is the relationship between democracy and national security?

There is a complex relationship between democracy and national security. On one hand, democracy can promote national security by creating a stable and resilient political system that is accountable to citizens and responsive to their needs. A democratic government that respects the rule of law, protects human rights, and fosters economic development can promote social stability and reduce the risk of internal conflict, terrorism, and other threats to national security. On the other hand, there are concerns that democracy can also create vulnerabilities in national security by making it more difficult to maintain secrecy, protect sensitive information, and respond quickly to emerging threats. Democratic governments are subject to public scrutiny and oversight, which can limit their ability to take swift and decisive action in response to national security challenges.

Furthermore, there are concerns that democratic processes can be manipulated or subverted by foreign powers or other actors seeking to undermine national security. This includes the use of disinformation campaigns, cyberattacks, and other forms of interference designed to disrupt democratic processes and sow division and mistrust within society.

Overall, the relationship between democracy and national security is complex and multifaceted, and it requires a careful balancing of competing priorities and concerns. Democratic governments must work to promote the values and institutions that underpin democracy while also ensuring that they are able to respond effectively to emerging threats and challenges to national security.

24. Explain the role of media in national security?

The media plays a crucial role in national security by providing information to the public and holding government officials accountable for their actions. In a democratic society, the media serves as a watchdog, providing a check on government power and ensuring that citizens are informed about key issues related to national security. One important role of the media in national security is to report on events and issues related to national security, including terrorism, military operations, and intelligence activities. By providing accurate and timely information to the public, the media can help to build public understanding and support for national security policies and actions.

Another important role of the media in national security is to serve as a check on government power. Through investigative reporting and critical analysis, the media can help to expose abuses of power, misconduct, and other issues that may compromise national security. At the same time, the media must also balance its role as a watchdog with its responsibility to avoid compromising national security. This requires careful consideration of the potential risks and consequences of reporting on sensitive information, such as classified intelligence or ongoing military operations.

Overall, the media plays a critical role in promoting transparency, accountability, and public understanding in matters related to national security. By providing accurate and timely information, holding government officials accountable, and ensuring that national security policies are consistent with democratic values and principles, the media helps to promote a safe and secure society for all.

25. Define the impact of propaganda on national security.

Propaganda can have a significant impact on national security by shaping public opinion, influencing decision-making, and creating division and mistrust within society. Propaganda refers to the dissemination of information, ideas, or opinions that are intended to influence or manipulate public opinion, often with a political or ideological agenda.

One impact of propaganda on national security is that it can create division and polarisation within society. By promoting a particular narrative or agenda, propaganda can create an "us versus them" mentality that can lead to social unrest, violence, and even civil conflict. This can undermine national unity and cohesion and make it more difficult to address common challenges and threats. Another impact of propaganda on national security is that it can create confusion and mistrust about government policies and actions. By spreading false or misleading information, propaganda can undermine public confidence in government institutions and erode support for national security measures. This can make it more difficult for governments to respond effectively to emerging threats and challenges.

Finally, propaganda can also be used as a tool of influence and manipulation by foreign powers or other actors seeking to undermine national security. By spreading disinformation, propaganda can create confusion, mistrust, and division within society, making it more difficult to maintain social stability and respond effectively to threats and challenges. Overall, the impact of propaganda on national security can be significant, and it requires careful monitoring and countermeasures to mitigate its negative effects. This includes promoting transparency and accountability in government policies and actions, fostering media literacy and critical thinking skills among the public, and countering false or misleading information through accurate and timely communication.

26. Define the concept of hybrid warfare.

Hybrid warfare is a form of conflict that combines traditional military tactics with unconventional methods, such as propaganda, cyberattacks, and economic pressure, to achieve strategic objectives. It is a complex and adaptive form of warfare that is characterised by its use of multiple domains and tactics, and its ability to operate below the threshold of conventional conflict.

Hybrid warfare is often used by state actors seeking to achieve their objectives without engaging in direct military conflict. By leveraging a variety of tools and tactics, such as disinformation campaigns, cyberattacks, and economic pressure, hybrid warfare can create strategic advantages and undermine the political and social stability of target countries. One key aspect of hybrid warfare is its ability to blur the lines between military and non-military activities. This makes it more difficult for target countries to respond effectively and may require new strategies and approaches to counter these threats.

Examples of hybrid warfare include Russia's annexation of Crimea in 2014, which involved a combination of military force, cyberattacks, and propaganda, and China's use of economic pressure and information warfare to advance its strategic objectives in the South China Sea. Overall, hybrid warfare represents a significant challenge to national security, as it requires new approaches and strategies to counter its complex and adaptive tactics. This includes improving intelligence capabilities, enhancing cyber defences, and building resilience to propaganda and disinformation campaigns.

27. Explain the role of Private Military Companies (PMCs) in modern warfare?

Private military companies (PMCs) are private companies that provide military services to governments, international organisations, or other clients. These services can include a wide range of activities, from logistics and training to combat operations and security services. One of the primary roles of PMCs in modern warfare is to fill gaps in military capabilities that are not provided by regular military forces. This includes tasks such as logistics, transportation, and security, as well as specialised services such as intelligence gathering and analysis. PMCs can also provide combat support services, such as tactical air support, that can enhance the capabilities of regular military forces.

Another role of PMCs in modern warfare is to provide security services in conflict zones or other high-risk environments. This can include protecting critical infrastructure, such as oil pipelines or mining operations, as well as providing security for humanitarian organisations or other clients.

However, the use of PMCs in modern warfare is not without controversy. Critics argue that PMCs can operate with less oversight and accountability than regular military forces, and that their actions can sometimes undermine human rights and international law. Additionally, the use of PMCs can create tensions with regular military forces, as well as with local populations and governments. Overall, the role of PMCs in modern warfare is a complex and evolving issue, and one that requires careful consideration of the benefits and risks involved. This includes ensuring appropriate oversight and accountability, as well as maintaining clear lines of authority and communication with regular military forces and other stakeholders.

28. State the impact of globalisation on military strategy?

Globalisation has had a profound impact on military strategy, as it has changed the nature of security threats and the ways in which military forces must respond to them. One of the key impacts of globalisation on military strategy is the increased importance of global security partnerships and alliances. As security threats become more complex and transnational, military forces must work together with other nations and organisations to address these challenges effectively.

Another impact of globalisation on military strategy is the increased use of technology and information. The rapid pace of technological advancement has created new opportunities and challenges for military forces, from the use of unmanned aerial vehicles (UAVs) and precision-guided weapons to the need for enhanced cyber defences and intelligence capabilities. Globalisation has also changed the nature of conflict, with many conflicts now taking place in urban environments or other densely populated areas. This requires military forces to adopt new tactics and strategies, such as precision targeting and the use of non-lethal weapons, to minimise civilian casualties and damage to infrastructure.

Finally, globalisation has also increased the importance of economic and cultural factors in military strategy. Military forces must consider the economic and social conditions that contribute to security threats, as well as the cultural and religious factors that can influence conflict dynamics and outcomes. Overall, the impact of globalisation on military strategy is complex and multifaceted and requires military forces to adapt to new challenges and opportunities to effectively address global security threats.

29. What is the relationship between nationalism and national security?

Nationalism and national security are closely related concepts, as both are concerned with the protection and preservation of a nation and its interests.

Nationalism refers to a strong sense of loyalty and identity towards one's nation, often characterised by a desire for self-determination and independence. Nationalism can play a key role in shaping national security policies, as it can motivate individuals to support and defend their country against perceived threats.

National security, on the other hand, refers to the protection of a nation's sovereignty, territorial integrity, and other vital interests. This includes both external threats, such as military aggression from other nations, and internal threats, such as terrorism or civil unrest. The relationship between nationalism and national security can be complex, as nationalist movements can sometimes challenge the authority of the state and undermine efforts to maintain national security. For example, nationalist movements seeking greater autonomy or independence can create tensions with the central government and lead to separatist movements, which can threaten national security.

However, nationalism can also be a powerful force for national unity and collective action in times of crisis. During times of war or other external threats, a strong sense of nationalism can help to mobilise the population and rally support for national security measures. Overall, the relationship between nationalism and national security is shaped by a variety of factors, including the nature of the threats facing a nation, the political and social context in which nationalist movements arise, and the ability of national leaders to effectively balance the interests of the state and the aspirations of the people.

30. How do ethnic and religious conflicts affect national security?

Ethnic and religious conflicts can have a significant impact on national security, as they can create divisions within a society and destabilise the political and social order. These conflicts can arise from a variety of factors, including historical grievances, economic disparities, and cultural and religious differences. One of the main impacts of ethnic and religious conflicts on national security is the potential for violence and civil unrest. When tensions between different ethnic or religious groups reach a critical point, they can lead to riots, protests, or even armed conflict, which can threaten the stability of the state and undermine the rule of law.

Ethnic and religious conflicts can also have economic and social impacts, as they can lead to displacement of populations, loss of property and livelihoods, and reduced investment and economic growth. This can further exacerbate the underlying grievances that give rise to the conflict and create new challenges for national security.

In addition to these direct impacts, ethnic and religious conflicts can also have broader regional and international implications, as they can spill over into neighbouring countries or attract the involvement of external actors. This can further complicate efforts to resolve the conflict and create new security threats for the state and the region. Overall, the impact of ethnic and religious conflicts on national security is significant and multifaceted and requires a comprehensive approach that addresses the underlying grievances and promotes social and economic development, as well as effective conflict resolution and peace-building efforts.

31. How do international organisations contribute to the maintenance of global security? OR How does the United Nations contribute to the maintenance of international security?

International organisations play a crucial role in maintaining global security by facilitating cooperation and coordination among countries on a range of security issues. These organisations are designed to address transnational challenges and threats that cannot be effectively addressed by individual countries acting alone. One of the main ways in which international organisations contribute to global security is by promoting international law and norms that govern state behaviour. Organisations such as the United Nations and its various agencies help to establish and enforce these laws and provide a framework for addressing violations and resolving disputes peacefully.

International organisations also facilitate collective action and cooperation among countries on a range of security issues, including conflict prevention and resolution, counterterrorism, and nuclear non-proliferation. By providing a platform for dialogue and collaboration, these organisations help to build trust and promote cooperation among countries, which can in turn contribute to the maintenance of global security.

In addition, international organisations provide a forum for countries to share information and intelligence, which can help to identify and respond to emerging security threats. By pooling resources and expertise, these organisations can also help to build capacity in countries that lack the resources or expertise to address security challenges on their own. Overall, the role of international organisations in maintaining global security is critical, as they provide a framework for collective action and cooperation among countries and help to establish and enforce international laws and norms that promote peace and stability.

32. Define the concept of deterrence in international relations.

In international relations, deterrence refers to the use of threats or military capabilities to prevent an adversary from taking a particular action. The aim of deterrence is to dissuade potential aggressors by convincing them that the costs of their actions will outweigh the benefits.

Deterrence operates on the principle of rational choice, if states will act in their own self-interest and that potential aggressors will be deterred if they believe that the costs of their actions will outweigh the benefits. The effectiveness of deterrence therefore depends on the credibility of the threat and the perceived costs and benefits of the potential action. There are two main types of deterrence: nuclear and conventional. Nuclear deterrence involves the threat of nuclear retaliation in response to an attack, while conventional deterrence involves the threat of military force or economic sanctions.

Deterrence is often seen as a key component of international security and stability, as it can help to prevent conflict and aggression by signalling resolve and dissuading potential aggressors. However, deterrence can also be destabilising if it leads to an arms race or creates a security dilemma, where one state's efforts to enhance its own security are perceived as a threat by other states. Overall, the concept of deterrence remains a central feature of international relations and continues to be a key consideration in the development of national security strategies and policies.

33. How do military doctrines influence defence policy development?

Military doctrines are sets of principles and guidelines that define how a military organisation operates, plans, and conducts operations. These doctrines can have a significant impact on defence policy development by shaping the military's approach to strategic planning, force structure, and capability development. By providing a framework for decision-making and action, military doctrines help to align military objectives with broader national security goals and objectives.

They also provide a basis for training, education, and professional development, ensuring that military personnel are prepared to execute their mission effectively. Military doctrines can also shape defence policy by influencing the allocation of resources and the development of new capabilities. For example, a doctrine that emphasises the importance of air power might lead to increased investment in air assets, while a doctrine that prioritises special operations might lead to increased investment in special forces capabilities.

Moreover, military doctrines can shape the way in which defence policy is communicated to the public and to other countries. By articulating clear objectives and explaining how those objectives will be achieved, military doctrines can help to build public support for defence policies and contribute to deterrence by signalling resolve and capability. Overall, military doctrines play an important role in shaping defence policy development by providing a framework for decision-making, influencing the allocation of resources and capability development, and helping to build public support and signal resolve.

34. How does military spending affect national security?

Military spending refers to the resources a government allocates towards the military, including salaries, weapons, equipment, and facilities. It is often considered a crucial factor in ensuring national security, as it enables a country to build and maintain a strong and capable military that can defend against external threats. However, the impact of military expenditures on national security is complex and multi-faceted.

On the one hand, military spending can enhance national security by providing resources for defence planning, preparedness, and the development of new technologies and capabilities. A strong military can serve as a deterrent against potential aggressors and provide a sense of security to citizens, which can contribute to social and political stability. On the other hand, excessive military spending can have negative effects on national security. High levels of military expenditures can divert resources away from other important areas, such as education, healthcare, and infrastructure, which can weaken a country's social and economic foundations. Moreover, military spending can contribute to national debt, which can constrain a government's ability to respond to future crises.

Additionally, excessive military spending can create security dilemmas and escalate arms races between countries, leading to heightened tensions and a greater risk of conflict. Thus, it is important to strike a balance between investing in military capabilities and maintaining other areas of national strength, such as education, healthcare, and infrastructure, to ensure long-term national security.

35. Why is maritime security important to national security?

Maritime security refers to the measures taken to ensure the safety and security of maritime trade and transportation, as well as the protection of national interests at sea. It is critical to national security because the sea is a crucial medium for international trade and commerce, and any disruption or threat to maritime security can have far-reaching consequences for a country's economy and security. Maritime security is essential for maintaining the free flow of goods and resources, including energy and raw materials, which are crucial to a country's economic well-being. A secure maritime environment also promotes stability and regional cooperation, which can contribute to the resolution of disputes and conflicts.

In addition, maritime security is important for safeguarding a country's borders and protecting against threats such as piracy, smuggling, and terrorism. These threats can have significant implications for national security, as they can undermine the rule of law and create instability in maritime regions.

Furthermore, maritime security is essential for ensuring the safety of maritime infrastructure, such as ports, harbours, and shipping lanes, which are critical to a country's economic and strategic interests. Any disruption to this infrastructure can have far-reaching consequences for a country's economy and security. In summary, maritime security is an integral part of national security, as it plays a critical role in maintaining the stability of the global economy, protecting against security threats, and safeguarding a country's interests at sea.

36. Define the concept of military strategy.

Military strategy is a set of plans, policies, and procedures developed by military leaders to achieve specific objectives in a given conflict or scenario. It is a complex and dynamic field that requires a deep understanding of military capabilities, as well as a comprehensive understanding of the political, economic, and social factors that may influence a conflict.

At its core, military strategy involves the development and deployment of military forces to achieve specific objectives, such as defending national borders, defeating enemy forces, or supporting allied forces in a conflict. This requires a careful assessment of the enemy's strengths and weaknesses, as well as an understanding of the military and political landscape in which the conflict is taking place. Military strategy also involves the allocation of resources, including personnel, weapons, and logistics, to achieve the desired objectives. This requires a careful balance between offensive and defensive capabilities, as well as a deep understanding of the enemy's capabilities and tactics.

In addition, military strategy often involves the use of intelligence gathering and analysis, as well as diplomatic and economic measures, to achieve the desired outcomes. This requires a comprehensive understanding of the political and economic factors that may impact the conflict, as well as the ability to adapt to changing circumstances and new developments. Overall, military strategy is a critical component of national security, as it plays a key role in ensuring the safety and security of a country and its citizens.

37. How do arms control treaties contribute to the prevention of nuclear weapons proliferation?

Arms control treaties play a critical role in preventing the proliferation of nuclear weapons. These agreements are designed to limit the spread of nuclear weapons and reduce the risk of nuclear war by establishing rules and regulations governing the possession, development, and use of these weapons. One of the key ways in which arms control treaties contribute to non-proliferation efforts is by establishing verification and monitoring mechanisms. These mechanisms allow treaty parties to monitor each other's compliance with the treaty provisions, thereby reducing the risk of cheating or violations.

Arms control treaties can also reduce the incentives for countries to acquire nuclear weapons. By limiting the number of nuclear weapons in the world and creating a taboo against their use, these treaties can make nuclear weapons less attractive as a tool of foreign policy or military strategy. In addition, arms control treaties can help build trust and confidence between countries. By engaging in negotiations and agreeing to common standards, countries can build relationships and reduce tensions, which can ultimately help to prevent conflicts and reduce the risk of nuclear war.

Overall, arms control treaties are an important tool in the effort to prevent nuclear weapons proliferation. By establishing rules and regulations, verifying compliance, reducing incentives for acquisition, and building trust between countries, these agreements help to create a more stable and secure world.

38. How do cyber-attacks affect national security?

Cyber-attacks pose a significant threat to national security, with potentially far-reaching and devastating consequences. The impact of cyber-attacks on national security can be wide-ranging, affecting critical infrastructure, government institutions, military operations, and the economy. One of the most significant impacts of cyber-attacks on national security is the potential disruption of critical infrastructure. Cyber-attacks on power grids, water supply systems, transportation networks, and other critical infrastructure can have catastrophic consequences, leading to widespread chaos and potentially putting lives at risk.

Cyber-attacks can also compromise national security by providing access to sensitive government and military information. Hackers may be able to steal classified information, compromise military networks, or gain access to sensitive diplomatic communications, putting national security at risk. In addition, cyber-attacks can have a significant impact on the economy, with potential consequences ranging from financial losses to market disruptions. Attacks on financial institutions, for example, can result in significant losses for individuals and businesses, while attacks on critical supply chains can disrupt commerce and industry.

Overall, cyber-attacks represent a significant threat to national security, with the potential for far-reaching and devastating consequences. Preventing and responding to these attacks requires a coordinated effort from government, military, and private sector entities, as well as ongoing investment in cybersecurity infrastructure and personnel.

39. Define the concept of war termination.

War termination refers to the process of bringing a conflict to an end, including the negotiations, agreements, and actions necessary to achieve a lasting peace. It involves a range of political, military, and social factors, and can take many forms, from the signing of a formal peace treaty to the gradual cessation of hostilities. Effective war termination requires careful planning and coordination to ensure that the conditions for a lasting peace are established. This may involve negotiating with the opposing side to establish a ceasefire, setting up transitional arrangements, and establishing mechanisms for conflict resolution and reconciliation.

One of the key challenges in war termination is the need to balance the competing interests and demands of different stakeholders. This may involve reconciling the goals of the military with those of the political leadership, ensuring the participation and representation of all relevant actors, and addressing the grievances and concerns of local communities and other affected parties.

The success of war termination efforts is often dependent on a range of factors, including the strength and capabilities of the parties involved, the nature of the conflict and the underlying causes, and the level of support and engagement from the broader international community. In summary, war termination is a complex and multifaceted process that involves a range of political, military, and social factors. It requires careful planning and coordination to achieve a lasting peace and can be influenced by a range of internal and external factors.

40. How does strategic culture influence the development of national security policy?

Strategic culture is the set of beliefs, values, and attitudes that shape how a country views its security and how it approaches strategic decision-making. Strategic culture is an important factor in the development of national security policy because it influences the country's perception of threats, its assessment of its own military capabilities, and its willingness to use force.

Different countries have different strategic cultures, which are shaped by factors such as their history, geography, political system, and military experience. For example, a country with a history of being invaded by its neighbours may have a more defensive strategic culture than a country that has not faced such threats. Similarly, a country with a strong tradition of civilian control of the military may be more cautious about using military force than a country where the military has a strong influence on policymaking. A country's strategic culture can also influence its approach to alliances and partnerships. A country that values self-reliance and independence may be less willing to enter into alliances or partnerships, while a country that values collective security may place more emphasis on building partnerships and alliances.

Therefore, understanding a country's strategic culture is important for policymakers as it helps in crafting policies that align with a country's security culture. The strategic culture can help in shaping a country's approach to international relations, and therefore, influence its decisions on whether to engage in conflicts, negotiate, or pursue other forms of diplomacy. In conclusion, strategic culture plays a crucial role in shaping national security policy and its development.

41. How are intelligence and military operations interconnected? OR What is the relationship between intelligence and military operations?

Intelligence and military operations are closely interconnected and are considered as two sides of the same coin. Intelligence gathering plays a crucial role in guiding military decision-making by providing information on the capabilities and intentions of adversaries, identifying potential threats, and highlighting opportunities for military action. In turn, military operations help to enable intelligence gathering by creating conditions for obtaining information, and by providing a means of verifying intelligence assessments.

Intelligence can influence the entire spectrum of military operations, including planning, execution, and evaluation. During the planning phase, intelligence provides the basis for determining the objectives of military operations and for developing the strategies to achieve those objectives. Intelligence also helps in identifying the capabilities and vulnerabilities of the adversary, which informs the selection of tactics and weapons. During the execution phase, intelligence provides the necessary situational awareness for commanders to make real-time decisions and adjust their plans. Intelligence enables the military to identify and target enemy forces, as well as identify potential threats and opportunities. It also helps in monitoring the progress of operations and adjusting plans as required.

Finally, in the evaluation phase, intelligence provides feedback on the effectiveness of military operations, which informs future decision-making. It helps to identify lessons learned and best practices, as well as highlighting areas for improvement. In conclusion, intelligence and military operations are mutually dependent and their cooperation is essential for effective military action. Intelligence provides the necessary information for military operations to be successful, while military operations enable the collection of information and validation of intelligence assessments.

42. How does terrorism affect the relationship between civilians and the military?

Terrorism can have a significant impact on the relationship between civilians and the military. In the aftermath of a terrorist attack, there is often a heightened sense of fear and a desire for increased security measures. This can lead to an expansion of the military's role in domestic affairs, such as increased involvement in counterterrorism efforts and the implementation of new security measures.

This increased involvement of the military in domestic affairs can have implications for civil-military relations. It may lead to a perception of the military as the primary protector of national security, potentially eroding the traditional separation between civilian and military roles. It may also lead to concerns about civil liberties and the potential for military overreach.

At the same time, terrorism can also lead to increased public support for the military and its role in protecting national security. This can strengthen civil-military relations by highlighting the importance of the military's role in defending the country against external threats. Overall, the impact of terrorism on civil-military relations depends on a variety of factors, including the severity of the threat, the response of the military, and the broader political and social context.

43. What is the role of military education in developing strategic thinkers?

Military education plays a crucial role in developing strategic thinkers. It prepares military officers to understand the complexities of national security challenges and provides them with the knowledge and skills needed to develop effective strategies to address those challenges. Military education programs are designed to promote critical thinking, strategic analysis, and decision-making skills. Students are taught how to evaluate information, identify key issues, and develop solutions that take into account the broader strategic context.

Military education also provides officers with an understanding of the political, economic, and social factors that shape national security policy. This broader understanding allows them to see how military actions fit into larger strategic goals and to think creatively about how military power can be used to achieve those goals. Military education is not only important for developing strategic thinkers but also for creating a common language and understanding among military officers from different services, branches, and countries. This helps to foster cooperation and coordination among military organisations and enables them to work together more effectively to achieve common objectives.

In addition to formal military education programs, many military officers also pursue advanced degrees in fields such as international relations, public policy, and business. This broadens their understanding of the larger strategic context and prepares them to work effectively with civilian policymakers and other stakeholders. Overall, military education is essential for developing the next generation of strategic thinkers and ensuring that military organisations are able to adapt to changing national security challenges.

44. What is the importance of defence industry in national security?

The defence industry plays a critical role in ensuring national security. It encompasses a broad range of activities, including research and development, production, and maintenance of military equipment and technologies. The importance of the defence industry in national security lies in its ability to provide the armed forces with the necessary tools to protect the nation from external threats. One of the primary benefits of a robust defence industry is that it can help reduce dependence on foreign suppliers. A country that can manufacture its own military equipment is better positioned to respond to national security threats than one that relies on foreign sources. The defence industry also contributes to the economy, creating jobs and generating revenue through exports.

The defence industry also plays an essential role in innovation. The development of cutting-edge military technology often requires significant investment, which the private sector is better equipped to provide than the government. The defence industry can leverage private sector investment to develop new technologies that can have both military and civilian applications, enhancing the nation's overall technological capabilities.

Moreover, the defence industry's research and development efforts can lead to technological advances that have far-reaching implications beyond national security. For example, the internet, GPS technology, and even duct tape all have their roots in military research and development. In summary, the defence industry's importance in national security stems from its ability to provide the necessary tools to protect the nation, reduce dependence on foreign sources, contribute to the economy, stimulate innovation, and produce technologies with civilian applications.

45. Define the concept of unconventional warfare.

Unconventional warfare is a military strategy that involves the use of tactics and techniques that are unconventional, irregular, or outside the norms of traditional warfare. It is often used by weaker powers or non-state actors to level the playing field against stronger opponents.

Unconventional warfare can take many forms, including guerrilla warfare, terrorism, sabotage, and espionage. It typically involves asymmetric warfare, in which one side has a significant advantage in terms of military resources and technology, and the other side relies on tactics such as surprise, deception, and mobility. The goal of unconventional warfare is often to wear down the enemy and undermine their morale and will to fight, rather than to achieve a decisive military victory. It may involve attacks on both military and civilian targets, with the aim of creating chaos and disrupting the enemy's ability to govern or operate effectively.

Unconventional warfare requires a high degree of flexibility and adaptability, as well as the ability to operate in small, decentralised units. It often involves close cooperation between military and civilian actors, including local communities and other non-state actors. Overall, unconventional warfare is an important strategy in modern military conflicts, as it allows weaker actors to challenge more powerful opponents and achieve their goals through unconventional means. However, it also raises significant ethical and legal questions, particularly when it involves attacks on civilian targets or the use of tactics that violate the laws of war.

46. What is the impact of modern information technologies on military operations?

Modern information technologies have had a significant impact on military operations, transforming the way wars are fought and won. These technologies have facilitated faster, more accurate communication and information sharing, enabling militaries to achieve greater situational awareness and improved decision-making capabilities.

One of the key impacts of modern information technologies on military operations has been the development of unmanned aerial vehicles (UAVs), also known as drones. UAVs provide militaries with a range of capabilities, including intelligence, surveillance, and reconnaissance (ISR), strike operations, and aerial refuelling. The use of drones has revolutionised modern warfare, allowing militaries to conduct precision strikes against targets without putting pilots in harm's way. Additionally, the use of advanced computing technologies, including artificial intelligence and machine learning, has enabled militaries to process and analyse vast amounts of data in real-time. This has resulted in improved situational awareness, more accurate predictions, and the ability to quickly respond to changing circumstances.

Furthermore, cyber warfare has emerged as a new domain of warfare, where information technologies play a critical role in disrupting or compromising the information and communication systems of the enemy. This has necessitated the development of defensive and offensive capabilities in cyber operations. In conclusion, modern information technologies have significantly impacted military operations, allowing militaries to operate more efficiently and effectively. As a result, it has become increasingly important for militaries to invest in these technologies to maintain their competitive edge and to ensure that they remain effective in the ever-changing landscape of modern warfare.

47. How does military intelligence contribute to the decision making process?

Military intelligence is an integral part of the decision-making process in the military. It involves the collection, analysis, and dissemination of information that is relevant to national security. Military intelligence helps decision-makers to understand the situation and the environment in which they are operating, to anticipate and identify potential threats, and to develop effective strategies to address them.

Military intelligence plays a critical role in the decision-making process by providing timely, accurate, and relevant information to decision-makers at all levels. It helps decision-makers to evaluate the strengths and weaknesses of their own forces and those of their adversaries. Additionally, military intelligence helps decision-makers to assess the effectiveness of their operations and to make necessary adjustments to ensure mission success.

The role of military intelligence in the decision-making process has become increasingly important in recent years, as the nature of warfare has changed. With the rise of asymmetric warfare and non-state actors, traditional military strategies are no longer effective. As such, military intelligence plays a critical role in helping decision-makers to develop new strategies and tactics that are better suited to modern conflicts. In summary, military intelligence is essential to the decision-making process in the military. It helps decision-makers to understand the situation and the environment in which they are operating, to identify potential threats, and to develop effective strategies to address them.

48. How does historical analysis contribute to the understanding of military strategy?

Historical analysis plays a crucial role in the understanding of military strategy by providing insights into the successes and failures of past military campaigns. By examining historical cases, military strategists can learn from the experiences of previous military leaders and apply those lessons to contemporary challenges. Historical analysis helps identify the strengths and weaknesses of different military strategies and tactics, allowing military planners to better anticipate and respond to future threats.

Moreover, historical analysis helps to develop a deeper understanding of the political and cultural contexts in which military operations take place. The study of history can help military planners identify key factors that can influence the outcome of a military campaign, such as the role of public opinion, the motivations of different actors, and the impact of technology on warfare. Furthermore, historical analysis also helps to identify patterns and trends in military strategy and tactics over time, enabling military planners to adapt their approaches to changing circumstances. It helps to develop a broader perspective that takes into account the complexity and interconnectedness of military and non-military factors that can influence the success or failure of military operations.

In short, historical analysis is important for understanding military strategy as it provides a wealth of information and insights that can inform military planning and decision-making. It helps to identify key factors that influence military operations, enables the adaptation of strategies to changing circumstances, and broadens the perspective of military planners beyond immediate concerns.

49. Define the concept of pre-emption in national security.

Pre-emption is a national security strategy that involves taking action to prevent an adversary from attacking by striking first. It is based on the belief that an enemy's attack is imminent or likely, and that a pre-emptive strike will be necessary to prevent the attack and protect national security interests. Pre-emption can involve military, diplomatic, or economic actions and can be used to counteract threats from conventional or non-conventional sources such as terrorism or cyberattacks.

Pre-emption is a controversial strategy, as it requires decision-makers to make difficult judgments about the likelihood and imminence of an adversary's attack, and the potential consequences of a pre-emptive strike. A pre-emptive strike can also be seen as an act of aggression, leading to retaliation from the targeted country and further escalation of the conflict. The concept of pre-emption has been used in various historical contexts, including the Cuban Missile Crisis in 1962, where the United States considered a pre-emptive strike on Cuba to prevent the Soviet Union from deploying nuclear missiles there. More recently, pre-emption has been used in the context of the War on Terror, with the United States taking pre-emptive military action against perceived terrorist threats in Afghanistan and Iraq.

Overall, pre-emption is a complex and controversial strategy that requires careful consideration of the potential risks and benefits, and the potential consequences for national security and international relations.

50. How does military technology influence the dynamics of the battlefield?

Military technology refers to the equipment, weapons, and systems developed for use by armed forces in battlefields. Over the years, military technology has significantly influenced the dynamics of the battlefield, shaping the way wars are fought. Modern military technology includes advanced drones, precision-guided munitions, cyber weapons, and other sophisticated systems.

The use of military technology enables a more efficient and effective projection of force, providing the military with an advantage in the battlefield. For example, drones can be used for surveillance, reconnaissance, and even targeted killings, allowing military forces to gather intelligence and engage enemy targets from a safe distance. Similarly, precision-guided munitions enable highly accurate targeting of enemy positions, reducing collateral damage and minimising the risk of friendly fire. Moreover, military technology has transformed the concept of the battlefield, blurring the lines between physical and cyber warfare. Cyber weapons, for example, can be used to disrupt enemy communications and disable critical infrastructure, rendering their conventional weapons and systems ineffective. As such, military technology plays a crucial role in shaping the dynamics of the battlefield and providing an edge in modern warfare.

In conclusion, military technology has revolutionised the way wars are fought, and its continued development and deployment will continue to influence the dynamics of the battlefield. Its importance cannot be overstated in ensuring national security and protecting the interests of the country.

51. How significant is strategic communication in the context of national security?

Strategic communication is a crucial element in national security policy. It refers to the coordinated use of communication methods and channels to convey information, influence attitudes, and achieve specific objectives. Effective strategic communication helps to shape perceptions, build trust, and rally support for government policies and actions.

In the context of national security, strategic communication serves several purposes. First, it helps to manage crises and mitigate potential conflicts by providing accurate and timely information to relevant stakeholders. Second, it can be used to counter misinformation and propaganda, which are increasingly used as weapons in contemporary conflicts. Third, it helps to build and maintain alliances by communicating shared values and goals. Moreover, strategic communication can also influence the behaviour of potential adversaries by demonstrating the capability and willingness to act if necessary. For example, military leaders may use strategic communication to convey messages of deterrence or warn of potential consequences for hostile actions.

Overall, strategic communication is an important tool for shaping the perception and behaviour of domestic and international audiences in the context of national security. It requires careful planning, coordination, and execution across different government agencies and media channels to achieve desired outcomes.

52. Define the concept of insurgency.

Insurgency refers to a form of violent and organised political rebellion against a constituted authority or government by a group of people who do not recognise the legitimacy of the current political regime. Insurgents aim to overthrow or replace the existing government, with the intention of establishing a new political system or implementing changes in the existing one.

Insurgencies are often characterised by the use of irregular tactics such as ambushes, hit-and-run attacks, and sabotage against military or government targets, as well as attacks on civilians or non-combatants who are seen as supporting the government. Insurgents often operate in a clandestine manner, blending in with the civilian population and using guerrilla warfare tactics to avoid detection and combat.

The causes of insurgency can vary, but they often include grievances related to political, social, economic, or ethnic issues. Insurgents may be driven by ideologies or beliefs that they feel are not represented or addressed by the existing government or political system. Insurgencies can be difficult to combat and often require a combination of military, political, and economic measures to address the root causes of the conflict. Effective counter-insurgency strategies typically involve a focus on winning over the hearts and minds of the local population, as well as disrupting and dismantling the networks that support the insurgency.

53. How do special operations forces contribute to modern warfare?

Special operations forces (SOF) play a crucial role in modern warfare. They are a highly trained, specialised group of military personnel who conduct covert or unconventional operations that require precision, flexibility, and speed. These operations can include intelligence gathering, reconnaissance, direct action, counterterrorism, and foreign internal defence.

SOFs operate in a wide range of environments, from urban areas to remote and hostile terrain. They are able to adapt quickly to changing situations and are capable of carrying out missions with minimal support. They work closely with other military units and government agencies to achieve strategic objectives and often play a critical role in achieving mission success. One of the key advantages of SOFs is their ability to operate in a low-profile manner, which makes them highly effective in conducting clandestine operations. Their training and equipment are tailored to the specific mission requirements, making them highly adaptable to different types of operations. They are often involved in highly sensitive missions, such as hostage rescue or targeted strikes against high-value targets.

Overall, SOFs have become an integral part of modern warfare. They are highly specialised, well-trained, and highly effective in achieving mission success. Their ability to operate in a low-profile manner and adapt quickly to changing situations makes them a key asset in the fight against terrorism and other threats to national security.

54. How do drone technologies affect military operations?

Drone technology has revolutionised modern military operations, allowing for greater precision and situational awareness on the battlefield. Drones, or unmanned aerial vehicles (UAVs), are used for a wide range of military missions, from surveillance and reconnaissance to targeted strikes against enemy forces.

One of the primary benefits of drone technology is the ability to conduct surveillance and gather intelligence on the battlefield without putting human pilots at risk. Drones can also provide real-time video and other data to commanders, enabling them to make more informed decisions about military operations. In addition, drones can be equipped with weapons, allowing for targeted strikes against enemy forces. This has become an increasingly popular tactic in modern warfare, particularly in counterterrorism operations.

However, the use of drone technology is not without controversy. Critics argue that the use of drones for targeted strikes raises ethical and legal questions, particularly when civilians are inadvertently killed or injured in these operations. The use of drones has also been criticised for its potential to undermine international law and norms around the use of force. Despite these concerns, drone technology is likely to continue to play an important role in modern military operations, particularly in counterterrorism and other asymmetric conflicts.

55. Why is the relationship between civilians and the military significant in democratic societies?

The relationship between civilians and the military is an essential component of democratic societies. Democratic governance requires the military to be under civilian control, and the civilian leaders must ensure that the military is used appropriately to protect the interests of the country and its people. Therefore, the relationship between civilians and the military must be based on mutual respect, trust, and cooperation.

Civil-military relations are important in democratic societies because they serve to safeguard the interests of citizens and prevent the military from becoming a threat to the democratic order. The military must always remain subservient to civilian authority, and it is essential to have mechanisms that ensure this principle is upheld.

Democratic societies require a military that is professional, disciplined, and respects human rights. Civilians are responsible for ensuring that military personnel are trained and equipped to defend the country, but also for ensuring that they respect the rule of law and human rights. Therefore, civilian oversight and accountability of the military are crucial to maintaining a professional and responsible military. The relationship between civilians and the military can also affect the morale and effectiveness of the military. If the military feels that it is not supported by the civilian leadership, or that it is being used for political purposes, then morale may suffer, and the effectiveness of the military may be compromised.

In summary, the relationship between civilians and the military is significant in democratic societies because it ensures that the military is under civilian control, that human rights and the rule of law are respected, and that the military is trained and equipped to defend the interests of the country and its people.

56. Define the concept of psychological warfare.

Psychological warfare is a form of warfare that aims to influence the thoughts, feelings, and behaviours of an adversary through the use of information, communication, and propaganda. This type of warfare involves the dissemination of information and messages to undermine the morale, confidence, and willpower of an enemy, in order to weaken their resistance and gain a strategic advantage.

Psychological warfare may include the use of various tactics such as disinformation, deception, misinformation, and propaganda. It can be conducted through a variety of media, including print, broadcast, and online media, as well as through personal contact and other forms of communication.

The goal of psychological warfare is to create a psychological climate that is favourable to achieving military objectives. It can be used to demoralise an enemy, create confusion and uncertainty, or to incite fear and panic. Psychological warfare can also be used to rally support for a military campaign or to counter propaganda efforts by the enemy. The use of psychological warfare is not limited to the military sphere, and it has been used by governments, political organisations, and other groups to achieve various objectives. However, its use is subject to ethical considerations, as it can involve the manipulation of information and the exploitation of vulnerabilities in an adversary.

57. *Briefly explain the use of gas warfare in the Second World War?*

Gas warfare, also known as chemical warfare, was extensively used in the Second World War by both the Axis and Allied powers. The use of poisonous gas in warfare began in the First World War and was prohibited by the 1925 Geneva Protocol, but this did not prevent its use in the Second World War.

The Nazis used poisonous gas to murder millions of people in concentration and extermination camps. They used hydrogen cyanide gas, known as Zyklon B, to kill prisoners in gas chambers. The gas was released into sealed chambers, causing death by suffocation. The use of gas was a highly efficient way to kill large numbers of people quickly and was a central aspect of the Nazi genocide. On the battlefield, the Axis powers also used poison gas, including mustard gas and nerve agents such as tabun and sarin. The Allies, on the other hand, did not use poison gas in combat, but they did conduct research and development of chemical weapons. In addition, they used propaganda about the potential use of gas as a deterrent against enemy forces.

The use of poison gas in the Second World War had a significant impact on the tactics and strategies of both sides. It caused widespread fear and created a need for gas masks and other protective gear. The use of gas also led to the development of countermeasures, such as gas detectors and protective clothing. The horrors of gas warfare led to the establishment of international agreements banning the use of chemical and biological weapons in warfare.

58. *Briefly explain the concept of city-states?*

City-states are independent political entities that consist of a single city and its surrounding territory. In ancient times, city-states were a common form of political organisation, particularly in Greece, where they emerged in the 8th century BCE. Each city-state had its own government, military, and economy, and they often engaged in trade and warfare with one another. City-states were usually small in size and population, with a few thousand to a few tens of thousands of residents. They were often ruled by a small group of elites, such as aristocrats or oligarchs, who held political power and controlled the city's resources.

City-states were influential in the development of democracy, as they were some of the first political entities to experiment with democratic governance. For example, Athens, one of the most famous city-states, is considered the birthplace of democracy. City-states were also significant in the spread of culture and ideas, as each city had its own unique traditions, customs, and practices. They often competed with one another in artistic and athletic events, such as the Olympic Games, which were held every four years in Olympia.

Today, city-states are less common as a form of political organisation, but some examples still exist, such as Singapore and Monaco.

59. Briefly explain the concept of indirect democracy?

Indirect democracy, also known as representative democracy or a republic, is a system of government where citizens elect representatives to make decisions and pass laws on their behalf. In this system, elected representatives are accountable to the people who elected them and are expected to represent their interests and concerns. In an indirect democracy, citizens exercise their political power through the act of voting. They elect representatives who serve in government institutions such as parliaments or congresses. These representatives are expected to work for the benefit of their constituents, as well as the wider population of the country.

The concept of indirect democracy has its roots in ancient Greece and Rome, where citizens elected representatives to govern on their behalf. It has since become the most common form of democracy around the world, as it allows for large and diverse populations to be represented through their elected officials.

Indirect democracy is often contrasted with direct democracy, where citizens directly participate in decision-making through initiatives, referendums, or town hall meetings. However, in practice, most modern democracies combine elements of both direct and indirect democracy.

60. Briefly explain the concept of lobbying?

Lobbying is the process of attempting to influence policymakers, usually elected officials or government bureaucrats, to take a specific course of action or support a particular position on an issue. It is a common practice in politics and involves individuals or groups who are interested in promoting their interests and agendas to government officials.

Lobbyists may work for corporations, non-profit organisations, interest groups, or other entities. They use a variety of tactics, such as providing information, organising events, and building relationships, to influence policymakers. Lobbying can take place at different levels of government, including local, state, and national.

One of the key aspects of lobbying is the ability to access and influence policymakers directly. Lobbyists use their knowledge of the political process, their understanding of the issues, and their relationships with policymakers to achieve their goals. They may also use campaign contributions or other means to influence policymakers.

Critics argue that lobbying can undermine democracy by giving undue influence to wealthy or powerful interests. However, supporters argue that lobbying is a legitimate form of political participation and that it allows individuals and groups to make their voices heard in the policymaking process. Ultimately, the effectiveness and legitimacy of lobbying depend on transparency and accountability, as well as the ethics and behaviour of lobbyists and policymakers.

61. How significant is the role of international law in controlling the application of force in the context of international relations?

International law plays a crucial role in regulating the use of force in international relations. The United Nations Charter, for instance, prohibits the use of force by one state against another except in cases of self-defence or with the approval of the United Nations Security Council. This principle is also reinforced by customary international law and other international agreements such as the Geneva Conventions.

International law provides a framework for countries to resolve conflicts peacefully through diplomacy and negotiation rather than resorting to military force. It creates a level playing field where all nations are expected to comply with the same rules and standards. This helps prevent powerful countries from using their military might to bully weaker nations.

Furthermore, international law helps protect civilians and other non-combatants from the devastating effects of armed conflict. It prohibits the use of certain weapons and tactics that can cause unnecessary suffering or damage to civilian populations. It also provides for the prosecution of war criminals and others who violate the laws of war. Overall, international law provides a critical means for regulating the use of force in international relations, promoting peaceful conflict resolution, protecting vulnerable populations, and promoting accountability for violations of the laws of war.

62. What is the concept of Grey Zone conflicts and their implications for national security?

Grey zone conflicts refer to ambiguous, non-traditional security challenges that fall somewhere between war and peace. These conflicts are characterised by the use of subversive tactics, such as disinformation campaigns, cyber attacks, and political influence operations, to achieve strategic objectives. Grey zone conflicts do not adhere to traditional rules of warfare, making them difficult to detect and respond to.

The implications of grey zone conflicts for national security are significant. Traditional military capabilities may not be effective in addressing these threats, as they often require more nuanced and creative responses. Grey zone conflicts also blur the lines between military and non-military actors, as non-state actors such as terrorist groups and criminal organisations become involved in these activities.

This can make it challenging for governments to determine the appropriate response and to ensure that their actions comply with international law. The use of grey zone tactics can also create confusion and uncertainty among the public, potentially eroding trust in government and democratic institutions. The spread of disinformation and propaganda can undermine social cohesion, fuel political polarisation, and exacerbate existing societal divisions. Therefore, it is crucial for governments to develop strategies to address grey zone conflicts and protect national security, while upholding democratic values and the rule of law.

63. Briefly explain the role and powers of India's Chief of Defence Staff (CDS)?

The Chief of Defence Staff (CDS) is the highest-ranking military officer in India, appointed as the principal military advisor to the government and the head of the newly created Department of Military Affairs (DMA). The role and powers of the CDS include:

1. <u>Strategic Planning</u>: The CDS is responsible for strategic planning and advising the government on matters related to defence. The CDS also provides advice on budgetary allocation for the military, military acquisitions, and modernisation plans.
2. <u>Jointness and Integration</u>: The CDS is expected to promote greater jointness and integration among the three services (Army, Navy, and Airforce) to achieve greater operational efficiency and effectiveness.
3. <u>Military Operations</u>: The CDS is responsible for the conduct of military operations and acts as the principal military adviser to the Prime Minister and the Cabinet Committee on Security in times of war or other military emergencies.
4. <u>Defence Procurement</u>: The CDS has been given the authority to prioritise and streamline the defence procurement process to reduce delays and ensure timely acquisition of critical defence equipment.
5. <u>Human Resource Management</u>: The CDS will oversee the creation of a new position of Joint Chief of Staff and provide advice on the management of military personnel, including promotions and postings.

The creation of CDS and the DMA represents a significant reform in India's national security structure, with the aim of promoting greater synergy and coordination among the three services and enhancing India's military capabilities. The CDS's powers are expected to help streamline decision-making, increase operational efficiency, and promote greater jointness and integration among the three services.

64. Briefly explain the objectives of India's National Security Guard (NSG)?

India's NSG (National Security Guard) was established in 1984 with the primary objective of countering terrorism, specifically responding to terrorist activities with a minimum possible loss of life and damage to public and private property. The NSG is a specialised force with a multi-dimensional role of performing both counter-terrorism and counter-sabotage activities

The main objectives of India's NSG include:

1. <u>To combat terrorism</u>: The NSG is primarily responsible for responding to terrorist activities and neutralising terrorist threats, both in India and

abroad.

2. <u>To undertake counter-hijacking operations</u>: The NSG is trained to respond to hijacking situations and conduct hostage rescue operations in case of an aircraft or other transport being hijacked.

3. <u>To provide specialsed training</u>: The NSG provides specialised training to other law enforcement agencies (State Police) and security forces in India.

4. <u>VIP security operations</u>: They also provide security to high-level dignitaries, including the President, Vice-President, and Prime Minister, as well as foreign dignitaries during their visits to India.

5. <u>Intelligence operations</u>: They also conduct intelligence operations to gather information on terrorist activities and potential threats.

Overall, the NSG plays a critical role in India's national security strategy, providing the country with a specialised force capable of responding to a range of security threats.

65. Briefly explain the Higher Defence Organisation of China?

The higher defence organisation of China is led by the Central Military Commission (CMC), which serves as the highest decision-making body on military affairs. The CMC is composed of two parts: the Central Military Commission of the Communist Party of China (CMC-CPC) and the Central Military Commission of the People's Republic of China (CMC-PRC). The Chairman of the CMC is the highest-ranking military officer in China, who also serves as the General Secretary of the Communist Party of China and the President of the People's Republic of China.

Below the CMC, there are four departments that oversee different aspects of the military: the General Staff Department (GSD), the Political Work Department (PWD), the Logistic Support Department (LSD), and the Equipment Development Department (EDD). These departments are responsible for planning, operations, logistics, and equipment development, respectively.

In addition to the CMC and its four departments, there are also seven military regions, which are responsible for the organisation and deployment of China's ground forces. Each military region is headed by a military commander, who is responsible for overseeing the troops in his region and reporting to the CMC. Overall, China's higher defence organisation is highly centralised, with the CMC at the top of the hierarchy and the various departments and military regions reporting to it. This system allows for efficient decision-making and command, but also raises concerns about potential abuse of power and lack of transparency.

66. Briefly explain the Higher Defence Organisation of India?

India's higher defence organisation is responsible for advising and assisting the government on matters related to national security, including military operations, defence policies, and the use of force. The organisation is headed by the Cabinet Committee on Security (CCS), which is chaired by the Prime Minister and includes the Minister of Defence, the Minister of External Affairs, the Minister of Home Affairs, and the Minister of Finance.

The CCS is supported by the National Security Council (NSC), which is responsible for strategic planning and policy coordination across various government agencies. The NSC is chaired by the Prime Minister and includes the National Security Advisor, the Chiefs of Staff of the Army, Navy, and Air Force, and other senior officials.

The Ministry of Defence (MoD) is responsible for the implementation of defence policies and the management of the armed forces. The MoD is headed by the Defence Minister and includes the Department of Defence, the Department of Defence Production, and the Department of Defence Research and Development. The Chiefs of Staff Committee (COSC) is the principal military advisory body to the government. It is headed by the Chief of Defence Staff (CDS), who is responsible for the overall management of the armed forces and the coordination of joint operations. The CDS is supported by the Integrated Defence Staff (IDS), which provides strategic planning and operational coordination across the three services.

In summary, India's higher defence organisation includes the CCS, NSC, MoD, COSC, CDS, and IDS, which work together to ensure effective decision-making and implementation of defence policies and strategies.

67. What are the needs for defence production?

Defence production refers to the manufacturing of weapons, equipment, and other military-related products that are used for the defence and security of a country. It is an essential aspect of national security, as the availability and readiness of defence products determine a country's ability to defend itself against any external threats. The need for defence production arises from the constant threat of wars, conflicts, and acts of terrorism that pose a significant threat to the security of a country. By having a strong and self-reliant defence production industry, a country can minimise its dependence on other countries for the supply of defence-related products, reduce costs, and ensure the timely availability of necessary equipment.

Defence production also plays a crucial role in boosting a country's economy by creating employment opportunities, generating revenue through exports, and promoting technological advancements. It also helps in the development of the indigenous defence industry, which contributes to the overall growth and progress of the country.

In addition, defence production is essential for maintaining a country's strategic autonomy and sovereignty. It enables a country to have control over its defence capabilities, ensuring that it can meet its national security needs independently and effectively.

Overall, defence production is a critical component of a country's defence strategy, and its importance cannot be overstated in maintaining national security, promoting economic growth, and ensuring strategic autonomy.

68. Briefly explain the merits and demerits of foreign sources in defence sector?

Foreign sources can provide both advantages and disadvantages to a country's defence production capabilities. Here are some of the merits and demerits of foreign sources in defence:

Merits

1. <u>Access to advanced technology</u>: One of the significant benefits of sourcing defence equipment and technology from foreign countries is the access to advanced and modern technology, which may not be available locally.

2. <u>Cost-effectiveness</u>: Foreign defence sources can provide cost-effective options as they benefit from economies of scale, which can be particularly helpful for countries with limited budgets.
3. <u>Speedy procurement</u>: Procuring defence equipment from foreign sources can sometimes be a quicker process as they are already manufactured and ready for use.
4. <u>Diversification</u>: Relying on foreign sources can help diversify a country's defence supply chain, reducing the risk of over-reliance on any single source.
5. <u>Strategic partnerships</u>: Sourcing defence equipment from a foreign country can lead to the development of strategic partnerships between the two countries, which can have broader economic and political benefits.

Demerits

1. <u>Dependency</u>: Over-reliance on foreign sources can make a country vulnerable to the policies and political changes of the source country. It can also lead to dependence on the source country's supply chain.
2. <u>National security concerns</u>: The use of foreign defence equipment raises national security concerns, particularly regarding the potential for the source country to have access to sensitive data and technology.
3. <u>Lack of customisation</u>: Defence equipment from foreign sources may not be customisable to meet specific requirements, leading to compromises on the country's defence strategy.
4. <u>Geopolitical implications</u>: Procuring defence equipment from a particular country may have geopolitical implications, and may impact relations with other countries or alliances.
5. <u>Economic benefits</u>: Over-reliance on foreign sources can lead to the loss of economic benefits associated with local defence production, including job creation and economic growth.

69. Explain in detail about Defence Planning in India since 1962?

Defence planning in India since 1962 has undergone several changes due to the evolving security environment and changing geopolitical realities. India's 1962 war with China highlighted the deficiencies in India's defence preparedness and triggered a series of reforms in India's defence planning process. The main objective of defence planning in India is to ensure that the country is adequately prepared to meet any security challenge that may arise.

In 1962, India established the Defence Planning Committee (DPC) to undertake a comprehensive review of the country's defence strategy and develop a long-term defence plan. In 1964, the DPC was replaced by the Defence Committee of the Cabinet (DCC), which remains the apex body for defence planning in India.

In the 1970s, India adopted a "forward policy" towards China, which involved deploying troops along the disputed border. This policy resulted in a military standoff with China in 1986-87 and led to a re-evaluation of India's defence strategy. The Kargil conflict in 1999 highlighted the need for better inter-service coordination and joint planning. The 1999 Kargil Review Committee recommended the creation of a Chief of Defence Staff (CDS) post to coordinate between the three services. In 2019, the CDS position was finally created, and the Integrated Defence Staff (IDS) was given the responsibility of preparing long-term defence plans and coordinating inter-service matters.

The Indian government has also adopted a "Make in India" policy, which seeks to promote domestic defence production and reduce India's dependence on foreign suppliers. This policy has resulted in the establishment of several defence manufacturing units in India.

In conclusion, India's defence planning process has evolved over the years to meet the changing security environment. The creation of the CDS position and the emphasis on joint planning and domestic defence production are significant steps towards enhancing India's defence preparedness.

70. What were the reasons for the partition of India and Pakistan?

The partition of India and Pakistan in 1947 was the result of a complex set of historical, social, economic, and political factors that had been building up for many years. Some of the major reasons for partition are:

1. <u>Political instability</u>: In the years leading up to partition, India was experiencing a period of political instability, with various factions and groups vying for power. The Indian National Congress and the All India Muslim League were the two main political parties, but they were unable to agree on how power should be shared.

2. <u>Economic disparities</u>: There were significant economic disparities between different regions of India, with some areas being much more prosperous than others. This had led to resentment and tensions between different communities.

3. <u>Violence and communal tensions</u>: As the idea of partition gained traction, there were outbreaks of communal violence between Hindus and Muslims, particularly in the regions that would later become Pakistan.

4. <u>Religious differences</u>: One of the main reasons for the partition was the religious differences between Hindu and Muslim communities. The idea of a separate Muslim homeland had been proposed by the All India Muslim League in the 1940s, and was supported by the British, who saw it as a way to divide and weaken India.

5. <u>British colonial rule</u>: The British had ruled India for nearly 200 years, and their policies had created deep divisions between various communities. They had also introduced a system of separate electorates for Muslims, which further reinforced the idea of separate identities.

Overall, the partition of India and Pakistan was a traumatic event that led to the displacement of millions of people and had long-lasting effects on the region.

71. Discuss the reasons for the refugee crisis in East Pakistan during 1970-71.

The refugee crisis in East Pakistan during 1970-71 was a result of various political, social, and economic factors that came together to create a volatile situation in the region. The crisis was primarily caused by the political tension between East and West Pakistan, economic disparities, and a lack of representation and autonomy for East Pakistan.

In the early 1970s, East Pakistan was politically and economically marginalised by the West Pakistani establishment, which controlled the central government. The people of East Pakistan were denied adequate representation and participation in the political process, and they felt that their voices were not being heard. Furthermore, the economic development of East Pakistan lagged behind that of West Pakistan, which caused widespread poverty and unemployment in the region.

The situation escalated in March 1971 when the military regime of Pakistan launched a brutal crackdown on the Bengali population of East Pakistan. The military's actions led to a mass exodus of refugees who fled across the border into India. The Indian government, which was already dealing with a refugee crisis in the region, was forced to intervene in the conflict to prevent further bloodshed and instability.

In summary, the refugee crisis in East Pakistan was a result of years of political, social, and economic marginalisation, as well as the brutal actions of the Pakistani military regime. The crisis ultimately led to the formation of the independent state of Bangladesh in December 1971.

72. What were the major events of the 1962 Sino-Indian War?

The Sino-Indian War of 1962 was a border conflict between India and China. Here are the major events of the war:

1. <u>Border disputes</u>: India and China had long-standing disputes over their shared border in the Himalayas, with both countries claiming the Aksai Chin region.
2. <u>Chinese invasion</u>: In October 1962, Chinese troops launched a surprise attack on Indian positions in the northeast and Ladakh region.
3. <u>Indian losses</u>: The Indian army was not prepared for the Chinese invasion, and suffered heavy losses in the early stages of the war.
4. <u>Chinese advances</u>: The Chinese army made rapid advances, capturing large areas of Indian territory, including the strategic town of Tawang in Arunachal Pradesh.
5. <u>Ceasefire</u>: The Chinese army made rapid advances, capturing large areas of Indian territory, including the strategic town of Tawang in Arunachal Pradesh.
6. <u>End of the war</u>: The war officially ended on November 21, 1962, with both sides agreeing to a ceasefire.
7. <u>Aftermath</u>: The Sino-Indian War was a major setback for India, which suffered territorial losses and a blow to its self-confidence. It also led to

a deterioration of relations between China and India, with the border dispute remaining unresolved to this day.

73. Provide a chronological outline of the Kargil war of 1999 and how Indian military emerged successful despite various challenges.

The Kargil War of 1999 was a significant armed conflict between India and Pakistan that took place in the Kargil district of Jammu and Kashmir. Here's a chronological outline of the key events of the war:

- May 3, 1999: The Indian Army discovers the presence of Pakistani infiltrators along the Line of Control (LoC) in Kargil.
- May 8, 1999: The Indian Army launches Operation Vijay to evict the infiltrators from Kargil.
- May 15, 1999: Indian Army captures strategic points of Tololing, Tiger Hill and Point 5140.
- June 5, 1999: The Indian Army recaptures Point 5140 from the Pakistani Army.
- June 7, 1999: The Indian Air Force launches Operation Safed Sagar to target Pakistani military positions in Kargil.
- June 13, 1999: An Indian MiG-21 aircraft is shot down by a Pakistani missile, leading to the capture of Indian Airforce pilot Flight Lieutenant K. Nachiketa.
- June 18, 1999: India launches Operation Khukri to rescue its soldiers who were surrounded by Pakistani forces in Himalayas.
- July 5, 1999: The Indian Army captures the strategic peak of Tiger Hill, leading to the fall of the Pakistani Army's positions in Kargil.

Despite the challenges faced by the Indian military, including harsh terrain, adverse weather conditions, and Pakistani troops occupying commanding heights, it emerged successful in the Kargil War. The Indian Army showed immense courage, determination, and strategic planning to evict the infiltrators and recapture the strategic peaks. The Indian Air Force played a vital role in providing air support to the ground troops, while the Indian Navy blockaded Karachi, preventing Pakistan from receiving supplies. The war also highlighted the need for better intelligence gathering and inter-service coordination in the Indian armed forces.

74. What are the different ways in which Kashmir question continue to affect India even today?

There are several ways in which the Kashmir issue continues to affect India:

1. <u>Security Threats</u>: The ongoing conflict in Kashmir has resulted in security threats for India. India has accused Pakistan of supporting terrorism in Kashmir, which has led to several terrorist attacks in the country.
2. <u>Diplomatic Tensions</u>: The Kashmir issue has also created diplomatic tensions between India and Pakistan. The two countries have had several border conflicts, and there have been instances of cross-border firing.
3. <u>Human Rights Concerns</u>: Indian government has been accused of human rights violations in Kashmir. There have been reports of excessive use of force by security forces, and restrictions on freedom of speech and movement in the region.
4. <u>Economic Losses</u>: The Kashmir issue has also had economic repercussions for India. The ongoing conflict has affected tourism, trade, and investment in the region.
5. <u>Political Unrest</u>: The Kashmir issue has also created political unrest in the country. There have been protests and demonstrations against the Indian government's policies in the region, and calls for greater autonomy for Kashmir.
6. <u>International Scrutiny</u>: The issue has attracted international attention and scrutiny. The United Nations (UN) has called for a peaceful resolution of the conflict, and several countries have expressed concern about the human rights situation in the region.

75. What according to Treaty Provision forbids attack on uninhabited land?

The concept of attacking uninhabited land is often referred to as "terra nullius" in international law, which means "nobody's land." According to treaty provisions, such an attack is forbidden as it violates the principle of territorial integrity of a state.

Under international law, every state has the right to territorial integrity, which means that its borders should be respected by other states. The United Nations Charter explicitly forbids the use of force against the territorial integrity or political independence of any state. This principle is also enshrined in various regional treaties, such as the Organisation of American States (OAS) Charter and the African Union (AU) Constitutive Act.

Moreover, the use of force against uninhabited land violates the principle of proportionality in the use of force. This principle requires that any use of force by a state should be proportionate to the threat it is facing. Attacking uninhabited land would be a disproportionate response to any perceived threat. In summary, attacking uninhabited land is forbidden under international law as it violates the principle of territorial integrity and the principle of proportionality.

76. What are the merits and demerits of codification of international law?

Codification of international law refers to the process of making international law more precise, consistent and accessible through the formulation of conventions, treaties, and customary rules. Here are some merits and demerits of codification of international law:

Merits

1. <u>Clarity and Consistency</u>: Codification of international law can make the legal framework clearer and more consistent. It can also help to reduce ambiguity and uncertainty, which is important for countries to comply with international law.
2. <u>Facilitation of Negotiations</u>: Codification can provide a useful framework for negotiations between states. It can help to identify common ground and areas of disagreement, and facilitate the resolution of disputes.
3. <u>Ease of Access</u>: Codification can make international law more accessible to all stakeholders, including states, individuals, and international organisations. It can also help to simplify the legal framework, making it easier for stakeholders to understand and apply.

Demerits

1. <u>Inflexibility</u>: The codification process can make international law less flexible and adaptive to changing circumstances. The rigid legal framework may not be able to address new issues that arise in international relations.
2. <u>Heterogeneous Interests</u>: The codification of international law may reflect the interests of the most powerful states, rather than the needs of all stakeholders. This can lead to unequal distribution of benefits and obligations under the law.
3. <u>Difficulty in Implementation</u>: Codification of international law does not necessarily ensure compliance by all states. Enforcement of international law is often difficult and depends on the willingness of states to adhere legal obligations.

In conclusion, while codification of international law has its merits, it is not a panacea for all international legal problems. It should be approached with caution and awareness of its potential limitations.

77. *Briefly explain the geostrategic location of Indian Ocean?*

The Indian Ocean is the third-largest ocean in the world and is bounded by Africa to the west, Asia to the north, Australia to the east, and the Southern Ocean to the south. It is an important geostrategic location due to its vast expanse and the presence of numerous important trade routes.

The Indian Ocean is a vital shipping lane that connects Europe, the Middle East, and Africa to Asia and Australia. It serves as a major passage for oil exports from the Persian Gulf to the rest of the world. The Strait of Hormuz, located at the entrance of the Persian Gulf, is a crucial chokepoint that controls the flow of oil from the Middle East.

The Indian Ocean is also home to a number of strategic islands, such as the Maldives, Mauritius, and the Seychelles, which provide important naval bases for various countries. India's Andaman and Nicobar Islands, located at the eastern entrance of the Indian Ocean, provide India with a strategic outpost in the region. The Indian Ocean is also of great geopolitical importance due to its proximity to various hotspots, such as the Persian Gulf, the Horn of Africa, and the South China Sea. It has been the site of various conflicts, including piracy and terrorism, and is a potential area of competition between major powers such as India, China, the United States, and Japan.

In conclusion, the geostrategic location of the Indian Ocean makes it a vital area of interest for various countries and has significant implications for global trade, security, and politics.

78. What is the concept of Fourth Generation Warfare and its implications for military strategy?

Fourth generation warfare (4GW) is a concept that describes a form of warfare characterised by the blurring of the lines between military and non-military actors, the use of irregular tactics such as terrorism and guerrilla warfare, and the use of propaganda and psychological operations to achieve political objectives. This form of warfare is often associated with asymmetrical conflicts in which a weaker non-state actor seeks to overcome a stronger state actor.

The implications of 4GW for military strategy are significant. Traditional military strategies that rely on overwhelming force and conventional tactics may be less effective in this type of conflict. Instead, a strategy that emphasises agility, flexibility, and adaptability is necessary to counter 4GW threats. This may involve a greater focus on intelligence gathering and analysis, as well as the development of specialised units and technologies to counter irregular tactics such as improvised explosive devices and suicide bombings.

Another important implication of 4GW is the importance of understanding the political, economic, and social dynamics of the conflict environment. Military forces must be able to work with local communities and governments to build trust and legitimacy, and to understand and address the root causes of the conflict. This requires a holistic approach that integrates military and non-military elements of national power, such as diplomacy, economic development, and humanitarian assistance.

In summary, the concept of 4GW challenges traditional notions of military strategy and requires a more nuanced and flexible approach to counter irregular threats. It emphasises the importance of understanding the political and social dynamics of conflict, and of integrating military and non-military elements of national power to achieve strategic objectives.

79. What is the impact of environmental degradation on national security?

Environmental degradation refers to the deterioration of the environment through depletion of resources, pollution, and destruction of ecosystems. This has significant implications for national security as it threatens the economic, social, and political stability of nations.

One of the most pressing environmental concerns that can affect national security is climate change. The rising sea levels, extreme weather events, and prolonged droughts can cause displacement, food and water scarcity, and conflicts over resources. These issues can exacerbate existing social and political tensions and even lead to violent conflicts.

Environmental degradation also affects the economic stability of nations. The depletion of natural resources such as forests, water, and minerals can cause economic shocks and destabilise markets. This can lead to poverty, unemployment, and social unrest. Environmental degradation can also affect national security by creating conditions that facilitate the spread of diseases. For example, deforestation and climate change can create conditions for the spread of infectious diseases, and poor water quality can lead to waterborne diseases.

To address these issues, national security policies need to incorporate environmental factors and prioritise sustainable development. This requires cooperation between governments, international organisations, and civil society to implement measures to protect the environment and mitigate the impacts of environmental degradation. Failure to do so can result in significant national security risks and undermine the stability and well-being of societies.

80. What is the concept of network-centric warfare and its implications for military operations?

Network-centric warfare is a concept that seeks to leverage advanced technologies and communication networks to enhance situational awareness, improve decision-making processes, and increase the efficiency and effectiveness of military operations. This approach emphasises the use of networked sensors, communication systems, and information technologies to enable real-time collaboration and sharing of information among military units, enabling them to act more quickly and effectively on the battlefield.

One of the main implications of network-centric warfare is that it requires a significant investment in advanced technologies and infrastructure. This can be both a benefit and a challenge, as it allows militaries to operate with greater precision and speed, but also requires significant resources to develop and maintain.

Another implication is that it can lead to a more decentralised approach to military operations, as information is shared more widely and decision-making is pushed down the chain of command. This can improve responsiveness and agility, but can also create challenges in terms of maintaining operational security and coherence. Overall, the concept of network-centric warfare represents a significant shift in military thinking and has the potential to revolutionise the way that wars are fought. However, it also raises important questions about the role of technology in warfare and the balance between centralisation and decentralisation in military operations.

81. What is the role of unmanned systems in modern warfare?

Unmanned systems, also known as unmanned aerial vehicles (UAVs) or drones, have increasingly become a significant part of modern warfare. The use of unmanned systems provides several advantages in military operations. Firstly, they reduce the risk of casualties to military personnel, enabling operations to be conducted remotely. Secondly, they can provide persistent surveillance over a target area, allowing for more effective monitoring of enemy activities. Thirdly, they can carry out precision strikes with minimal collateral damage.

Unmanned systems can also be used for a range of military purposes, including reconnaissance, surveillance, target acquisition, and combat. In recent years, the development of unmanned systems has also led to the emergence of new types of military operations, such as swarm attacks, where a large number of drones are coordinated to attack a target.

However, there are also challenges associated with the use of unmanned systems in warfare. One of the primary concerns is the potential for unintended consequences and civilian casualties, particularly when using armed drones. Additionally, there are concerns about the ethics of using unmanned systems in warfare, particularly as the technology continues to advance and becomes more autonomous.

Overall, the use of unmanned systems in modern warfare offers a range of advantages but also presents ethical, legal, and strategic challenges that need to be carefully considered.

82. How has the concept of deterrence evolved since the end of Cold War?

The concept of deterrence has undergone significant changes since the end of the Cold War. During the Cold War, deterrence was primarily focused on nuclear weapons and the idea of mutually assured destruction (MAD). However, with the end of the Cold War and the reduced emphasis on nuclear weapons, the concept of deterrence has expanded to include a wider range of security threats, including terrorism, cyber attacks, and conventional warfare.

One of the most significant changes in the concept of deterrence is the move away from purely military means of deterrence to a more comprehensive approach that includes economic and diplomatic measures. This approach, sometimes referred to as "comprehensive deterrence," recognises that a state's security is affected by a range of factors beyond just military strength.

Another important development in the concept of deterrence is the growing recognition of the importance of regional and international cooperation in deterrence efforts. This includes alliances, partnerships, and cooperative security measures aimed at deterring common threats.

Finally, the concept of deterrence has also evolved to include the idea of "extended deterrence," which involves the use of a state's military capabilities to deter threats to its allies or partners. This has become increasingly important as the nature of threats to international security has become more diffuse and transnational.

Overall, the concept of deterrence has evolved to become more comprehensive and nuanced since the end of the Cold War, with a greater emphasis on non-military measures, cooperation, and extended deterrence.

83. What is the impact of global pandemics on national security?

Global pandemics have significant impacts on national security, with their effects extending beyond the public health domain. The sudden emergence of infectious diseases, such as COVID-19, can overwhelm national health systems, disrupt critical infrastructure, cause economic and social dislocation, and exacerbate political instability.

One of the immediate effects of a pandemic is the potential to disrupt critical infrastructure such as supply chains, transportation, and communication systems. The sudden cessation of such systems can lead to the collapse of the economy and social dislocation. Additionally, pandemics can exacerbate political instability as governments are forced to divert resources from other areas to deal with the crisis. This diversion can lead to a weakening of institutions, which can then result in the inability of governments to provide basic services and security to their citizens.

Moreover, pandemics can impact national security by creating opportunities for criminal organisations to exploit the chaos and confusion caused by the pandemic. For example, during the COVID-19 pandemic, there has been an increase in cyber-attacks targeting critical infrastructure, such as hospitals and research facilities, by criminal organisations seeking to exploit vulnerabilities in the system.

In conclusion, pandemics have significant impacts on national security, and it is crucial for governments to take a comprehensive approach to deal with them. This approach should include measures to strengthen critical infrastructure, improve public health systems, and enhance international cooperation to prevent future pandemics.

84. Define the concept of "grey swans" in national security.

The term "grey swans" refers to potential events or crises that are not certain to occur but have a significant impact on national security if they do. These events are different from "black swans," which are unexpected and improbable events with high impact.

Grey swans can include events such as natural disasters, economic collapses, cyberattacks, and geopolitical tensions that have a high probability of occurring and can significantly affect national security. These events are challenging to predict and prepare for, as they can have unpredictable and cascading effects on various sectors, making them a significant challenge for policymakers and security planners.

Grey swans pose a unique challenge to national security because they require flexibility in response and preparedness. The ability to adapt quickly to changes in the security environment is crucial to addressing grey swan events. Developing contingency plans and implementing measures to mitigate potential risks can help reduce the impact of such events.

Overall, grey swans require a proactive and holistic approach to national security planning that takes into account a broad range of potential scenarios and their potential impacts. By doing so, policymakers can help prevent or mitigate the risks of grey swans and promote national security in a rapidly changing and uncertain world.

85. Define the concept of "lethal autonomy" in military technology.

"Lethal autonomy" is the concept of granting weapons and military technology the ability to make lethal decisions without human intervention. It is the idea of creating machines that can operate on their own, decide targets, and engage in military operations, without human supervision or intervention.

The development of autonomous weapons has the potential to revolutionise warfare, providing advantages such as increased accuracy, speed, and reduced risk to military personnel. However, the concept of lethal autonomy also raises serious ethical and legal concerns. The lack of human oversight and control could result in machines making decisions that violate human rights, international humanitarian law, and the principles of just war.

The deployment of autonomous weapons could also result in an increased likelihood of accidental conflict escalation or unintended harm to civilians. Additionally, the lack of accountability and responsibility for actions taken by autonomous weapons could undermine the principle of individual and state responsibility, which is crucial for maintaining the international legal order.

The concept of lethal autonomy raises critical questions about the balance between military necessity and ethical considerations in warfare. Therefore, it is essential for policymakers, military leaders, and society as a whole to engage in a dialogue about the development and deployment of autonomous weapons and to establish ethical, legal, and policy frameworks to ensure that lethal autonomy is deployed in a manner that conforms to international law, human rights, and the principles of just war.

86. Define the concept of "deep fakes" in information warfare.

Deep fakes refer to manipulated digital content, such as images or videos, that are created using artificial intelligence (AI) and machine learning techniques. These manipulations are often so convincing that they are difficult to distinguish from real content. Deep fakes can be used for malicious purposes, such as spreading disinformation, propaganda, or blackmail.

In the context of information warfare, deep fakes pose a significant threat as they can be used to spread false information and manipulate public opinion. Deep fakes can be created to impersonate political figures, celebrities, or other individuals to make them appear to say or do something they did not. This can be used to spread false information or to damage the reputation of the individual being impersonated.

Deep fakes can also be used to create fake news stories or manipulate news footage, leading to the spread of misinformation and propaganda. They can be used to amplify existing tensions or to create new conflicts between different groups, leading to increased instability and unrest.

Overall, the concept of deep fakes highlights the growing threat of technology-based disinformation and the need for increased awareness and countermeasures to protect against it. It is important for governments, organisations, and individuals to be aware of the potential impact of deep fakes and to take steps to identify and combat their use.

87. What is the impact of commercialisation of space on national security?

The commercialisation of space has significant implications for national security as it provides new opportunities for innovation and access to resources that could enhance the military capabilities of states. However, it also poses several challenges for traditional security strategies and raises questions about how to manage potential conflicts and risks.

On one hand, the commercialisation of space has led to increased investment in space technology, which has created opportunities for the development of advanced communication and surveillance systems, and enhanced intelligence gathering capabilities. Commercial satellite imagery and GPS technology are widely used by militaries around the world, and space-based assets are integral to modern warfare. Private companies are also developing innovative solutions for space exploration, transportation, and resource exploitation, which could have significant applications for national security.

On the other hand, the commercialisation of space also creates new vulnerabilities and challenges for traditional security strategies. With increasing numbers of private entities entering the space domain, there is a risk of commercial activities interfering with military operations or disrupting strategic systems. The proliferation of space debris and the potential for collisions also poses a risk to space-based assets and could impact national security. Additionally, the private ownership of space resources and infrastructure raises questions about sovereignty and regulation, and the potential for conflict over resources. In summary, the commercialisation of space has significant potential to enhance national security through increased access to advanced technology and resources, but it also poses new risks and challenges that must be managed effectively.

88. What is the impact of water scarcity on regional security?

Water scarcity can have a significant impact on regional security as it can lead to conflicts between nations, communities, and individuals. Water is a vital resource for human survival and economic growth, and its scarcity can lead to tensions and conflicts over access, distribution, and use.

In regions where water resources are limited or unevenly distributed, disputes over water can arise, leading to tensions and conflicts between countries. The competition for water resources can exacerbate existing political and economic tensions, especially in regions where water is scarce or there is a lack of infrastructure to manage water resources.

Water scarcity can also lead to social unrest within countries. In areas where water is limited, people may be forced to migrate, leading to social and economic instability. The lack of water can also lead to health issues, such as the spread of water-borne diseases, which can further exacerbate social tensions. In addition to these security implications, water scarcity can also have economic consequences. Water scarcity can lead to reduced agricultural productivity, which can impact food security and increase food prices. It can also impact industrial output, as many industries require large quantities of water for production.

In conclusion, water scarcity can have significant implications for regional security, economic stability, and social harmony. Therefore, it is crucial for policymakers to prioritise the management and allocation of water resources to prevent tensions and conflicts arising from water scarcity.

89. Define the concept of "bunker busters" in military technology.

"Bunker busters" are military weapons designed to penetrate deep into the ground or reinforced structures to destroy underground installations such as military bunkers, tunnels, and command centres. They are specifically designed to defeat hardened and deeply buried targets that traditional explosives and conventional bombs cannot penetrate.

These weapons can be conventional bombs, missiles, or special penetrator warheads designed to break through concrete, steel, or rock. They typically use a combination of high explosive and kinetic energy to penetrate the target and then detonate the explosive payload inside. They can cause significant collateral damage due to their high explosive power and can pose a risk to nearby civilian populations.

Bunker busters have been used in various conflicts, including the Gulf War, the Iraq War, and the conflict in Afghanistan. The use of bunker busters has raised ethical and legal concerns, particularly regarding the risk of civilian casualties, as they are often used in urban areas.

Overall, the development and use of bunker busters reflect the increasing emphasis on precision-guided munitions and the use of advanced technology in modern warfare. However, their use also underscores the need for careful consideration of the humanitarian and ethical implications of such weapons in military operations.

90. What is the concept of "just war theory" and its relevance to modern warfare?

Just War Theory is a moral and ethical framework that seeks to determine when the use of military force is justified, and how it can be conducted in a manner that is consistent with moral principles. It is a concept that dates back to ancient times and has evolved over time to reflect changing norms and values. The theory has two main components: jus ad bellum, which deals with the justification for going to war, and jus in bello, which deals with the conduct of war.

According to just war theory, military force can be used only in defence of an attack or to prevent an imminent attack, as a last resort, after all other options have been exhausted, and with proportionality, meaning the harm caused by the military action should not be greater than the harm it seeks to prevent.

The relevance of just war theory in modern warfare lies in its ability to provide a moral and ethical framework for the use of military force. It helps to ensure that military actions are not taken lightly and that they are conducted in a manner that is consistent with moral principles. It also provides a basis for holding leaders accountable for their decisions to go to war and the conduct of the war.

However, there are criticisms of just war theory, such as the subjectivity in determining what is just and the potential for abuse by those in power. Some argue that the theory is outdated and needs to be adapted to reflect changing norms and values, such as the rise of non-state actors and the increasing role of technology in warfare.

91. Define the concept of "Greymail".

"Greymail" is a tactic used in legal and national security contexts, in which a defendant threatens to reveal classified or sensitive information in order to force the government to drop charges or offer a favourable plea deal. The term "greymail" comes from the combination of "greymail" (a legal tactic of threatening to expose embarrassing information in order to gain a strategic advantage) and "blackmail."

The basic idea behind greymail is that by threatening to disclose sensitive information, the defendant hopes to create a dilemma for the government: either proceed with the prosecution and risk exposing classified information in court, or drop the charges and avoid the risk of disclosure. This tactic can be particularly effective in cases involving national security, where the government may be hesitant to disclose classified information in open court.

Greymail can be seen as a form of legal blackmail, in which the defendant uses the threat of disclosure to gain leverage in legal negotiations. Critics argue that this tactic undermines the rule of law and national security, by allowing defendants to manipulate the legal system for their own benefit. Overall, the use of greymail highlights the challenges of balancing the need for transparency and accountability with the need to protect national security and sensitive information.

92. What is the impact of political polarisation on military operations?

Political polarisation can have a significant impact on military operations in several ways. Firstly, it can lead to a lack of political consensus on key national security issues, such as the deployment of troops or the allocation of resources to the military. This can result in delayed or ineffective decision-making, which can have severe consequences for military operations.

Secondly, political polarisation can create an environment in which the military becomes politicised and divided, with factions aligning themselves with different political parties or ideologies. This can lead to a breakdown in discipline and command structures, as well as a loss of morale and focus among troops.

Thirdly, political polarisation can lead to a lack of public support for military operations, particularly in cases where there is a perception that the military is being used for political purposes rather than for genuine national security reasons. This can make it harder for the military to achieve its objectives and can also put troops in danger by exposing them to greater levels of hostility and resistance from local populations.

Overall, political polarisation can have a detrimental impact on military operations by undermining decision-making, creating division within the military, and eroding public support for military action. It is therefore important for political leaders to prioritise national security over political considerations and work towards building consensus on key issues.

93. What is the impact of the Fourth Industrial Revolution on military operations?

The Fourth Industrial Revolution (4IR) is characterised by the fusion of technologies that blur the lines between the physical, digital, and biological spheres. This technological revolution is expected to have a significant impact on the way militaries operate. The impact of 4IR on military operations can be seen in several areas:

1. <u>Data-driven Decision-Making</u>: 4IR technologies such as artificial intelligence, machine learning, and big data analytics can provide the military with valuable insights that can aid in decision-making.
2. Unmanned Systems: The use of unmanned systems such as drones, unmanned ground vehicles, and unmanned underwater vehicles can provide the military with enhanced situational awareness and the ability to operate in environment that are hazardous to human operators.
3. Cyberwarfare: 4IR technologies such as artificial intelligence and machine learning can be used to develop advanced cyber weapons that can target critical infrastructure and disrupt military operations.
4. Additive manufacturing: Additive manufacturing or 3D printing can provide the military with the ability to produce critical parts and equipment on-demand, reducing the logistical burden of maintaining large stockpiles of spare parts.

However, the adoption of 4IR technologies also brings challenges. The reliance on technology can create vulnerabilities that can be exploited by adversaries. The use of unmanned systems also raises ethical and legal concerns. Additionally, the integration of 4IR technologies into existing military structures and processes requires significant investment in training and infrastructure.

In summary, the impact of the Fourth Industrial Revolution on military operations is significant, providing both opportunities and challenges that must be carefully managed to ensure that the military remains effective in a rapidly changing environment.

94. *What is the impact of the COVID-19 pandemic on military readiness and operations?*

The COVID-19 pandemic has had a significant impact on military readiness and operations worldwide. Military personnel, like other essential workers, are at high risk of infection, and the pandemic has disrupted military operations, training, and deployments.

One of the major impacts of the pandemic on military readiness has been the implementation of COVID-19 protocols. These protocols include social distancing, face coverings, and reduced personnel on bases and ships, which have affected military readiness by limiting the availability of personnel and restricting training opportunities. Additionally, travel restrictions have resulted in canceled or postponed deployments and exercises, affecting the readiness of units that were scheduled to deploy. The pandemic has also resulted in changes in the way military operations are conducted. Military planners have had to adapt to the pandemic's impact by changing operational plans, conducting more virtual meetings, and reducing in-person interactions. The pandemic has highlighted the need for more flexible and adaptable military planning and operations.

The pandemic has also increased the demand for military assistance in responding to the pandemic. The military has played a significant role in supporting civil authorities by providing medical personnel, equipment, and logistical support. The pandemic has highlighted the importance of military capabilities in responding to crises and disasters.

Overall, the pandemic has had a significant impact on military readiness and operations. However, the military has adapted to the pandemic's challenges, and the experience has highlighted the need for more adaptable and flexible military planning and operations.

95. What is the concept of "fifth-generation warfare" and its implications for national security?

The concept of "fifth-generation warfare" refers to a new paradigm of warfare that is characterised by the use of non-traditional tactics, including the manipulation of information, disinformation campaigns, cyber-attacks, and subversion of societal structures. Unlike traditional warfare, the focus of fifth-generation warfare is not on military force, but rather on the ability to influence the target population's perceptions and behaviours.

The implications of fifth-generation warfare for national security are significant. Unlike traditional warfare, where the state's military is the primary line of defence, fifth-generation warfare is conducted primarily by non-state actors such as hackers, social media influencers, and propaganda outlets. This means that the traditional tools of national defence, such as military hardware and intelligence-gathering, may be less effective in countering this new threat.

Furthermore, the use of fifth-generation warfare tactics by hostile foreign powers can result in the destabilisation of a target state's political and social structures, which could have long-lasting consequences. It is also difficult to attribute attacks to specific actors, making it hard to determine the appropriate response.

To address the challenges posed by fifth-generation warfare, national security strategies must evolve to include new tools and tactics that can effectively counter these non-traditional threats. This may include strengthening cybersecurity, investing in new technologies to detect and combat disinformation campaigns, and improving the ability to quickly respond to attacks on critical infrastructure.

96. What is the concept of "dark data" and its implications for military intelligence analysis?

The concept of "dark data" refers to information that is collected and stored by organisations, but is not actively used for analysis or decision-making. In the context of military intelligence analysis, dark data can include information from a variety of sources, such as intercepted communications, satellite imagery, and social media posts, that is not fully exploited due to technical, organisational, or cultural barriers.

The implications of dark data for military intelligence analysis are significant. First, the failure to effectively exploit all available data can result in incomplete or inaccurate assessments of threats, capabilities, and intentions of potential adversaries. This can lead to strategic and operational failures, including missed opportunities and unexpected losses on the battlefield.

Second, the presence of dark data can also pose significant security risks. Unsecured or unmanaged data can be vulnerable to cyber-attacks, insider threats, and other forms of unauthorised access, potentially leading to the compromise of sensitive military intelligence information.

To address these challenges, military intelligence organisations must adopt new technologies and methods for data collection, storage, and analysis that enable the effective exploitation of all available information. This may include the use of artificial intelligence and machine learning to automatically identify relevant data points, as well as the development of new processes and procedures for data management and analysis.

Additionally, organisations must prioritise the security of their data, implementing robust security protocols and training personnel to recognise and mitigate potential security threats.

97. What is the impact of the rise of autocratic regimes on global security?

The rise of autocratic regimes has significant implications for global security. Autocratic regimes are characterised by a concentration of power in the hands of a single leader or small group of elites, often with little regard for democratic institutions or individual rights. This can lead to a range of destabilising actions, including aggressive foreign policies, human rights abuses, and support for extremist groups.

One of the primary impacts of autocratic regimes on global security is the erosion of international norms and institutions. Autocratic leaders may disregard treaties, agreements, and norms that are designed to promote cooperation and prevent conflict, leading to increased tensions and a breakdown of diplomatic relations. Additionally, autocratic regimes may support extremist groups, providing funding, weapons, and other support that can fuel conflicts and instability in other regions.

The rise of autocratic regimes also has implications for the global balance of power. Autocratic leaders may seek to expand their influence in their region or beyond, potentially leading to conflicts with other states. Additionally, autocratic regimes may pursue aggressive military policies, such as the development of nuclear weapons or the expansion of military capabilities, that can further destabilise global security.

To address the challenges posed by the rise of autocratic regimes, the international community must work to promote democratic values and institutions, while also recognising the need to engage with autocratic leaders to promote stability and prevent conflict. This may include a range of diplomatic, economic, and military measures designed to deter aggression and promote cooperation.

98. Define the concept of "strategic empathy" in military diplomacy.

The concept of "strategic empathy" in military diplomacy refers to the ability of military leaders to understand and appreciate the perspectives, motivations, and interests of their counterparts in other countries. This involves a willingness to see the world from the other side's point of view, to understand their concerns and priorities, and to communicate effectively in ways that build trust and promote cooperation.

Strategic empathy is an essential component of effective military diplomacy, as it allows leaders to build relationships with their counterparts based on mutual respect and understanding. By demonstrating empathy, military leaders can create an environment of trust and openness, which can be critical to resolving conflicts and addressing shared security challenges.

At its core, strategic empathy requires military leaders to be active listeners, to seek out the views and perspectives of their counterparts, and to be willing to engage in constructive dialogue even in the face of disagreement. This approach can help to build common ground and identify areas of shared interest, while also promoting understanding and respect for different viewpoints. Strategic empathy can also be a valuable tool for conflict prevention, as it can help military leaders to identify potential areas of tension before they escalate into full-blown conflicts. By understanding the concerns and interests of their counterparts, military leaders can work to address underlying issues before they become more serious.

Overall, strategic empathy is a key component of effective military diplomacy, helping to build trust, promote cooperation, and prevent conflicts. By fostering an environment of mutual understanding and respect, military leaders can work to promote global stability and security.

99. Define the concept of "strategic foresight" and its implications for military planning.

The concept of "strategic foresight" refers to the ability of military planners to anticipate and prepare for future security challenges, by identifying potential threats, opportunities, and emerging trends that may impact global security. Strategic foresight involves a range of analytical tools and methods, including scenario planning, trend analysis, and horizon scanning, that allow military planners to think creatively and strategically about the future.

The implications of strategic foresight for military planning are significant. By anticipating future security challenges, military planners can develop more effective strategies and capabilities that are better aligned with future needs. This can help to avoid costly mistakes and ensure that military resources are being used effectively. Additionally, strategic foresight can help to identify opportunities for innovation and collaboration. By understanding emerging trends and technologies, military planners can work to leverage new capabilities and build partnerships that enhance their effectiveness and resilience.

Strategic foresight can also help military planners to identify potential vulnerabilities and risks, and to develop contingency plans and response strategies that can be activated quickly in the event of a crisis. By being prepared for a range of possible scenarios, military planners can ensure that they are able to respond effectively to unexpected events.

Overall, the concept of strategic foresight is essential for effective military planning, enabling military leaders to anticipate future challenges and opportunities, and to develop strategies and capabilities that are better aligned with future needs. By adopting a strategic foresight approach, military planners can help to ensure that their organisations are better prepared for the uncertain and complex security environment of the future.

100. Explain the concept of "algorithmic warfare" and its implications for national security?

The concept of "algorithmic warfare" refers to the use of advanced algorithms and machine learning techniques to enhance military operations and decision-making processes. Algorithmic warfare can involve a range of applications, including predictive analytics, autonomous systems, and cyber operations, and is aimed at increasing the speed, accuracy, and efficiency of military operations.

The implications of algorithmic warfare for national security are significant. By leveraging advanced algorithms and machine learning techniques, military forces can gain a decisive advantage over their adversaries, by processing and analysing large volumes of data more quickly and accurately than humans could ever do. At the same time, the use of algorithmic warfare raises a range of ethical and legal concerns. The deployment of autonomous systems and the use of predictive analytics can have unintended consequences, such as the potential for civilian casualties or the exacerbation of existing social and economic inequalities.

Moreover, the use of algorithms and machine learning systems can introduce new vulnerabilities and risks, such as the potential for cyber attacks or the manipulation of data to undermine the integrity of military operations.

To address these challenges, military forces must take a holistic approach to algorithmic warfare, carefully considering the ethical, legal, and strategic implications of these technologies. This may involve a range of measures, including the development of robust governance frameworks, the establishment of clear lines of accountability, and the investment in technologies that enhance the transparency and explainability of algorithmic systems. Ultimately, the responsible use of algorithmic warfare can help to enhance national security, while also protecting the rights and interests of all stakeholders involved.

101. Explain the concept of "biodefence" and its relevance to national security?

The concept of "biodefence" refers to the set of measures and strategies employed by governments and other organisations to protect against the deliberate or accidental release of biological agents that could pose a threat to public health or national security. Biodefence involves a range of activities, including the detection and surveillance of potential biological threats, the development of countermeasures and treatments, and the establishment of response plans and protocols.

The relevance of biodefence to national security is significant. Biological agents have the potential to cause widespread harm and disruption, affecting not only public health but also critical infrastructure, the economy, and social stability. Moreover, the intentional use of biological agents by state or non-state actors could have far-reaching geopolitical consequences, leading to conflict, instability, and even war.

Effective biodefence requires a multi-faceted approach, involving the cooperation and coordination of multiple stakeholders, including government agencies, international organisations, and the private sector. This may involve the development of advanced detection technologies, the investment in research and development of new treatments and vaccines, and the establishment of response plans and protocols that are adaptable and resilient.

Moreover, biodefence also requires a sustained commitment to public education and engagement, as well as international cooperation and coordination, to address the global nature of the biological threat. By investing in biodefence and working together to address this critical security challenge, governments and other organisations can help to protect public health and safety, promote global stability, and enhance national security.

102. Explain the impact of the rise of populism on global security?

The rise of populism has significant implications for global security. Populism is a political ideology that emphasises the interests and needs of the common people over those of the elite or establishment. Populist leaders often appeal to emotions and nationalistic sentiments, and their policies are characterised by a rejection of international cooperation and a focus on national sovereignty.

One of the key impacts of populism on global security is the potential for increased instability and conflict. Populist leaders often take an aggressive stance towards other countries, and their policies may lead to a breakdown in diplomatic relations and the erosion of established international norms and institutions. This can create a sense of uncertainty and unpredictability, increasing the likelihood of miscalculations, misunderstandings, and ultimately, conflict. Furthermore, the rejection of international cooperation and the emphasis on national sovereignty can lead to a weakening of multilateral institutions and mechanisms, which play a critical role in promoting global security. Populist leaders may prioritise their domestic interests over international obligations, which can undermine efforts to address transnational threats such as climate change, terrorism, and nuclear proliferation.

Populism also has implications for the protection of human rights and the rule of law, which are fundamental to global security. Populist leaders may seek to limit freedom of speech, restrict the rights of minorities, and undermine democratic institutions, which can erode the foundations of stable and peaceful societies.

To address the challenges posed by populism, it is essential for governments and other stakeholders to promote dialogue, cooperation, and engagement across borders. This may involve a renewed emphasis on the importance of international institutions and the rule of law, as well as efforts to address the underlying social, economic, and political factors that contribute to the rise of populism.

103. How can the military contribute to the promotion of sustainable energy management in regions affected by conflict?

The military can play a significant role in promoting sustainable energy management in conflict-affected regions. One way is through the deployment of renewable energy technologies in military operations, which can reduce the reliance on fossil fuels and minimise the environmental impact of military activities. This can include the use of solar panels, wind turbines, and other forms of renewable energy to power military installations and operations.

In addition, the military can work with local communities to develop sustainable energy infrastructure, such as micro-grids and off-grid energy systems. This can help to improve access to reliable and affordable energy for local populations, which can have a positive impact on social and economic development.

The military can also support efforts to address the root causes of conflict by promoting sustainable energy management as a means of improving environmental sustainability and reducing resource scarcity. This can involve working with local communities to develop sustainable land use practices, promoting the use of energy-efficient technologies, and supporting efforts to reduce greenhouse gas emissions. Furthermore, by promoting sustainable energy management, the military can contribute to the development of a more stable and secure environment. Access to energy is essential for economic development, and promoting sustainable energy management can help to reduce the risk of resource-related conflict, which can contribute to regional instability.

Overall, the military has a critical role to play in promoting sustainable energy management in conflict-affected regions, which can have positive impacts on both the environment and the well-being of local communities.

104. How does the increase in authoritarianism affect global security and democracy?

The rise of authoritarianism poses significant challenges to global democracy and security. Authoritarian leaders often prioritise their own interests over those of their citizens, and may use repressive tactics to maintain power, including limiting freedom of speech, restricting access to information, and suppressing dissent. This can erode the foundations of democratic societies and undermine the protection of human rights.

Moreover, the rise of authoritarianism can lead to a breakdown in international cooperation, as authoritarian leaders may prioritise their own national interests over those of the international community. This can lead to a weakening of multilateral institutions and mechanisms, which play a critical role in promoting global security and addressing transnational challenges such as climate change, terrorism, and nuclear proliferation.

The erosion of democratic norms and institutions can also lead to increased social and political polarisation, which can contribute to instability and conflict. Authoritarian leaders may seek to exploit these divisions for their own gain, leading to a breakdown in social cohesion and a rise in political extremism.

Furthermore, the rise of authoritarianism can have economic implications, as authoritarian regimes may prioritise short-term gains over long-term sustainability. This can lead to a lack of investment in critical areas such as education, healthcare, and infrastructure, which can have negative impacts on social and economic development.

Overall, the rise of authoritarianism poses significant challenges to global democracy and security, and underscores the importance of promoting democratic values and institutions both at home and abroad. This requires a renewed commitment to multilateralism and international cooperation, as well as efforts to address the underlying social, economic, and political factors that contribute to the rise of authoritarianism.

105. Explain the Gandhian approach and its relevance today in conflict resolution?

The Gandhian approach to conflict resolution is based on the principles of nonviolence, truth, and moral courage. This approach seeks to address conflicts through nonviolent means, including peaceful protests, civil disobedience, and dialogue. Gandhi believed that nonviolence was not only a moral imperative but also a strategic necessity, as it could help to mobilise broad-based support and create a moral force that could overcome even the most powerful opponents.

Today, the Gandhian approach remains relevant as a tool for conflict resolution, particularly in situations where traditional military or diplomatic approaches may not be effective. Nonviolent resistance has been used to bring about significant social and political changes, including the end of colonialism in India, the civil rights movement in the United States, and the overthrow of authoritarian regimes in countries such as Tunisia and Egypt. Nonviolent resistance can also be an effective tool for resolving conflicts at the local level, including disputes over land, resources, and other issues. By promoting dialogue and engagement, nonviolent resistance can help to build bridges between communities and foster greater understanding and trust.

Moreover, the Gandhian approach to conflict resolution can also help to address the root causes of conflict, including social and economic inequality, corruption, and injustice. By promoting transparency and accountability, and by empowering marginalised communities, nonviolent resistance can help to create a more just and equitable society, which can contribute to greater stability and security in the long term.

Overall, the Gandhian approach to conflict resolution remains relevant today as a tool for promoting nonviolent solutions to conflicts at all levels, from the local to the global. By emphasising the importance of nonviolence, dialogue, and moral courage, this approach offers a powerful alternative to traditional military and diplomatic strategies, and provides a framework for building more peaceful and just societies.

106. Examine the initiatives and effectiveness of CBMs between India and Pakistan.

Confidence-building measures (CBMs) have been an important component of India-Pakistan relations since the 1980s, with the aim of reducing tensions and promoting dialogue between the two countries. However, the effectiveness of these measures has been limited, and their impact on the overall relationship has been minimal.

One of the most significant CBMs between India and Pakistan has been the ceasefire along the Line of Control (LoC) in Kashmir, which was agreed upon in 2003. While the ceasefire has been largely successful in reducing cross-border violence and improving the security situation in the region, violations of the ceasefire by both sides continue to occur, and there have been several major escalations of violence in recent years. Other CBMs, such as the opening of trade and travel routes between the two countries, have also had limited impact, due to ongoing political tensions and security concerns. The visa liberalisation agreement, which was signed in 2012, has been subject to frequent suspensions and restrictions, while the opening of the Wagah-Attari border for trade has been hampered by bureaucratic hurdles and infrastructure constraints.

Moreover, the impact of CBMs has been further limited by the lack of progress on more substantive issues, such as the status of Kashmir, terrorism, and water-sharing. Without progress on these core issues, the impact of CBMs is likely to remain limited, and the risk of renewed conflict between the two countries will remain.

Overall, while CBMs have played a role in reducing tensions between India and Pakistan, their effectiveness has been limited, due to ongoing political and security concerns, as well as the lack of progress on more substantive issues. To achieve lasting peace and stability in the region, it will be necessary to address these underlying issues and to promote greater dialogue and cooperation between the two countries.

107. Discuss various challenges to India's foreign policy in South Asia?

India's foreign policy in South Asia faces several challenges that impede its efforts to establish greater regional influence and stability. Some of these challenges include:

1. <u>China's growing influence</u>: China's increasing economic and military presence in South Asia, particularly in countries such as Pakistan, Sri Lanka, and Nepal, poses a significant challenge to India's regional influence.
2. <u>Terrorism:</u> Cross-border terrorism originating from Pakistan and other countries in the region has been major challenge for India's foreign policy. This has also contributed to strained relations between India and Pakistan.
3. <u>Border Disputes</u>: India faces ongoing border disputes with several neighbouring countries, including China, Pakistan, and Bangladesh, which can lead to tensions and instability in the region.
4. <u>Political Instability</u>: Several countries in the region, such as Afghanistan, Bangladesh, and Sri Lanka, have experienced political instability in recent years, which has made it difficult for India to build stable relationships with these countries.

5. <u>Economic challenges</u>: Economic disparities and dependence on foreign aid in many South Asian countries limit India's ability to engage in economic diplomacy and build mutually beneficial relationships.
6. <u>Domestic political challenges</u>: Domestic political challenges in India, such as tensions between different ethnic and religious groups, can also impede its efforts to build stronger relationships with its neighbours.

In order to overcome these challenges, India must work towards building more inclusive and stable relationships with its neighbours, and continue to pursue policies that promote economic development and regional stability. It will also need to engage in constructive dialogue with China and other regional powers, while maintaining a strong focus on countering cross-border terrorism and addressing border disputes.

108. What is the significance of great game in Afghanistan?

The Great Game refers to the rivalry between the British and Russian empires in Central Asia during the 19th century. Afghanistan, which is strategically located between the two empires, was at the centre of this rivalry. Both the British and the Russians saw Afghanistan as a key buffer state that could protect their respective empires from each other.

During this period, the British sought to expand their influence in Afghanistan and prevent the Russians from doing the same. They fought several wars with the Afghan rulers, including the First and Second Anglo-Afghan Wars. The Russians also sought to gain influence in Afghanistan, and in the late 19th century, they signed a treaty with the Afghan rulers to establish closer ties. The Great Game had significant implications for Afghanistan, as it resulted in the country becoming a pawn in the power struggle between the British and the Russians. It also had implications for the region as a whole, as it helped to shape the political and strategic landscape of Central Asia.

Today, the legacy of the Great Game continues to shape Afghanistan's relationship with its neighbours and the wider international community. The country's strategic location, as well as its natural resources and geopolitical importance, make it a key player in the region. The ongoing conflict in Afghanistan can also be seen as a continuation of the Great Game, as regional and international powers seek to assert their influence over the country.

109. Describe the different political systems followed by the South Asian countries?

The South Asian region comprises of several countries, each with its own unique political system. The different political systems followed by South Asian countries are:

1. <u>India</u>: India is a federal parliamentary democratic republic, where the President is the head of state and the Prime Minister is the head of government.
2. <u>Pakistan</u>: Pakistan is a federal parliamentary democratic republic, where the President is the head of state and the Prime Minister is the head of government.
3. <u>Bangladesh</u>: Bangladesh is a parliamentary democratic republic, where the President is the head of state and the Prime Minister is the head of government.
4. <u>Sri Lanka</u>: Sri Lanka is a semi-presidential representative democratic republic, where the President is the head of state and the Prime Minister is the head of government.
5. <u>Nepal</u>: Nepal is a federal parliamentary democratic republic, where the President is the head of state and the Prime Minister is the head of government.
6. <u>Bhutan</u>: Bhutan is a constitutional monarchy, where the King is the head of state and the Prime Minister is the head of government.
7. <u>Maldives</u>: Maldives is a presidential representative democratic republic, where the President is the head of state and the head of government.

Despite the differences in their political systems, all these countries face similar challenges in terms of political instability, corruption, and economic development. However, there have been efforts to strengthen democratic institutions and promote good governance in the region, which have led to some progress in these areas.

110. What are the key highlights in India-Maldives relationship?

India-Maldives relations have been characterised by historical, cultural, and economic ties, as well as strategic concerns. Some of the key highlights of the relationship are:

1. <u>Strategic Partnership</u>: In 2019, the two countries signed a bilateral agreement to establish a Strategic Partnership, which aimed to deepen cooperation in areas such as defence, security, trade, and tourism.
2. <u>Development Assistance</u>: India has provided significant development assistance to the Maldives, including the construction of several key infrastructure projects such as the international airport, a hospital, and a cricket stadium. India has also provided financial assistance to support the Maldives' economic development.
3. <u>Political Cooperation</u>: India and the Maldives have cooperated closely on political issues, including the promotion of democracy, regional security, and counter-terrorism. India has been supportive of the Maldives' transition to democracy in recent years.
4. <u>Cultural Ties</u>: India and the Maldives have strong cultural ties, with the Maldives being a predominantly Muslim country and India being a predominantly Hindu country. There is also a significant population of people of Maldivian origin in India.
5. <u>Maritime Security</u>: Given their proximity to each other, India and the Maldives have cooperated closely on maritime security issues, including piracy and illegal fishing. The two countries have signed several agreements to enhance cooperation in this area.

Overall, the India-Maldives relationship has been characterised by close cooperation and mutual support, with both countries recognising the importance of the relationship for their respective strategic interests.

111. *Explain the non-traditional security threats confronting India-Bangladesh relationship?*

India and Bangladesh share a complex and multifaceted relationship, with non-traditional security threats being a major challenge. Some of the non-traditional security threats confronting India-Bangladesh relationship are:

1. <u>Illegal Migration</u>: The issue of illegal migration from Bangladesh to India has been a source of tension between the two countries. India has

accused Bangladesh of not doing enough to stop illegal migration, while Bangladesh has accused India of harassing Bangladeshi migrants.

2. <u>Terrorism</u>: Both India and Bangladesh have faced terrorist threats from extremist groups, such as the Islamic State (IS) and Al Qaeda in the Indian Subcontinent (AQIS). There have been concerns that these groups may use the porous border between India and Bangladesh to carry out attacks.

3. <u>Transnational Organised Crime</u>: India and Bangladesh have also faced challenges from transnational organised crime, such as drug trafficking, human trafficking, and smuggling. The border between the two countries is often used by criminal networks to carry out illegal activities.

4. <u>Climate Change</u>: Climate change is a significant non-traditional security threat facing both India and Bangladesh. Rising sea levels and increased frequency of extreme weather events have the potential to displace millions of people, leading to refugee crises and increased tensions between the two countries.

5. <u>Water Security</u>: The sharing of rivers between India and Bangladesh is a contentious issue, with concerns about the impact of upstream dams on downstream water flows. The two countries have signed several agreements to manage water resources, but disputes over water sharing continue to be a source of tension.

Overall, addressing these non-traditional security threats is crucial for ensuring a stable and peaceful relationship between India and Bangladesh. Both countries need to work together to find solutions to these challenges and promote regional security and cooperation.

112. Is Military - Media relationship complimentary or confilctual? Discuss.

The relationship between the military and the media is often complex and multifaceted, with both complementary and conflictual elements.

On the one hand, the military and media can have complementary interests. For example, the military may use the media to disseminate information about its activities and achievements to the public, while the media may use the military as a source of news and information. In this sense, the military and media can have a symbiotic relationship, where each benefits from the other. On the other hand, the military and media can also have conflicting interests. For example, the military may seek to control the narrative about its activities and may view the media as a threat to its authority and reputation. Conversely, the media may seek to hold the military accountable and may view the military as a source of potential wrongdoing and abuse of power.

In recent years, there have been several instances where the military and media have come into conflict, such as when the military has sought to control the reporting of conflicts or when the media has reported on military abuses of power. These conflicts can undermine public trust in both institutions and can lead to a breakdown in communication and cooperation.

Ultimately, the relationship between the military and media is complex and context-dependent. While there are certainly areas of complementarity, there are also areas of potential conflict. Finding ways to balance these interests and promote open and transparent communication between the military and media is crucial for ensuring public trust and promoting democratic accountability.

113. How the brain-mapping technology can be used for military operations?

Brain-mapping technology is a rapidly advancing field that has the potential to revolutionise a range of industries, including military operations. By using brain-mapping technology, it is possible to understand and decode the activity of different regions of the brain, allowing for more accurate prediction and manipulation of behaviour and decision-making.

In military operations, brain-mapping technology could be used in a variety of ways. For example, it could be used to enhance the performance of soldiers, by identifying areas of the brain that are associated with particular skills or abilities and training soldiers to activate those areas more effectively. It could also be used to identify and treat mental health conditions such as post-traumatic stress disorder (PTSD) in military personnel.

Another potential application of brain-mapping technology in military operations is in the area of enhanced interrogation. By understanding the neural activity associated with certain thought processes or emotions, it may be possible to manipulate these processes to extract information from enemy combatants more effectively. However, the use of brain-mapping technology in military operations also raises a range of ethical and legal concerns. For example, there are questions about the legality of using brain-mapping technology to extract information from prisoners of war. There are also concerns about the potential for misuse of the technology, such as the use of brain stimulation to control or manipulate individuals against their will.

Overall, while brain-mapping technology has the potential to be a powerful tool in military operations, its use must be carefully considered and regulated to ensure that it is used in a responsible and ethical manner.

114. Write about the scope of Peace and Conflict Studies?

The field of peace and conflict studies is an interdisciplinary field of study that explores the root causes of conflict, the dynamics of violent and nonviolent conflict, and the conditions necessary for peace-building and conflict resolution. The scope of peace and conflict studies is vast, encompassing a range of disciplines, theories, and practices.

At the heart of peace and conflict studies is a focus on understanding the nature of conflict and violence, and identifying ways to prevent, manage, and resolve conflicts. This involves studying the political, economic, social, and cultural factors that contribute to conflict, as well as the different approaches to conflict resolution and peace-building that have been developed over time.

The scope of peace and conflict studies also includes exploring the role of individuals, communities, and institutions in promoting peace and preventing violence. This involves examining the ways in which social and political structures can be transformed to promote peace and justice, as well as the role of international institutions and organisations in mediating conflicts and promoting peace.

Overall, the scope of peace and conflict studies is broad, encompassing a range of theoretical, practical, and interdisciplinary approaches. By bringing together scholars and practitioners from different disciplines and backgrounds, the field of peace and conflict studies seeks to develop a deeper understanding of the nature of conflict and violence, and to identify effective strategies for building peace and promoting social justice.

115. Explain the Communist approach to war?

Communist approaches to war are guided by Marxist-Leninist ideology, which seeks to abolish capitalism and establish a socialist society. Communists view war as an extension of class struggle, with the bourgeoisie using war to protect their interests and exploit the proletariat. Therefore, communists see the need to engage in war in order to defend the interests of the working class and advance the cause of socialism.

The communist approach to war emphasises the importance of ideological struggle, with the belief that propaganda and political education are essential tools for mobilising the masses and building support for the revolution. Communists also believe in the importance of a strong, disciplined military force, which is seen as a key instrument for defending the revolution and advancing the cause of socialism.

In practice, communist approaches to war have taken various forms, ranging from guerrilla warfare to conventional military operations. Communist guerrilla warfare has been used successfully in several revolutionary struggles, with the focus on hit-and-run tactics, mobility, and surprise attacks. Communist regimes have also pursued ambitious military modernisation programs, such as the Soviet Union's focus on building a powerful army during the Cold War.

Overall, communist approaches to war emphasise the importance of political and ideological factors, and the role of the military in advancing the cause of socialism. While these approaches have been successful in some contexts, they have also been criticised for their emphasis on ideological purity and political control, which can lead to authoritarianism and human rights abuses.

116. Do you think that Indian Armed Forces are capable of facing its adversaries? Critically analyse.

The Indian Armed Forces are one of the largest militaries in the world, with more than 1.4 million active personnel. The military has played an essential role in securing India's territorial integrity and defending its sovereignty. However, the question of whether the Indian Armed Forces are capable of facing its adversaries is a complex one and depends on several factors.

Firstly, the Indian Armed Forces are equipped with modern weaponry and have undergone significant modernisation in recent years. The military has acquired new fighter jets, attack helicopters, missile systems, and other advanced equipment. These advancements have significantly improved the military's capabilities and have enabled it to be better prepared for any potential threats. Secondly, the Indian Armed Forces have a high level of training and experience, having been involved in several conflicts, including the 1999 Kargil War and numerous counter-insurgency operations. The military has a significant advantage over its adversaries in terms of training, discipline, and tactical experience.

However, there are also some challenges that the Indian Armed Forces face. The military's procurement process is often slow, leading to delays in acquiring new equipment and weapons. There are also concerns regarding the military's organisational structure and coordination between different branches of the armed forces.

Furthermore, the military's budget has been a point of concern, with some experts arguing that the military's budget is not sufficient to address the current security challenges faced by the country adequately. In conclusion, while the Indian Armed Forces have made significant advancements in recent years, there are still some challenges that need to be addressed to ensure the military is fully capable of facing its adversaries. It is essential to continue to modernise the military, improve coordination between different branches, and ensure adequate funding for defence.

117. Is the use of nuclear weapons ever justified in modern warfare?

The use of nuclear weapons is a highly debated issue, and there is no clear consensus on whether it can ever be justified in modern warfare. Proponents of nuclear weapons argue that they are necessary to deter aggression and maintain international security, while opponents argue that the devastating effects of nuclear weapons make their use unjustifiable under any circumstance.

One of the main arguments in favour of the use of nuclear weapons is that they can serve as a deterrent to potential aggressors, thereby preventing conflict and maintaining peace. However, opponents argue that the use of nuclear weapons would result in catastrophic consequences that would far outweigh any potential benefits. The indiscriminate and long-lasting effects of nuclear radiation can cause immense suffering and devastation for generations to come.

Furthermore, the use of nuclear weapons would violate the principles of just war theory, which requires that military force be used only as a last resort, and that the harm caused by the use of force must be proportionate to the goal being pursued. Given the immense harm that would be caused by the use of nuclear weapons, it is difficult to argue that their use would ever be proportionate to any legitimate military objective.

In conclusion, the use of nuclear weapons is a complex issue that requires careful consideration and analysis. While some may argue that their use can be justified in certain circumstances, the overwhelming consensus among policymakers and scholars is that the use of nuclear weapons would be unjustifiable and morally reprehensible under any circumstance.

118. Should military spending be decreased to allocate more funds for social welfare programmes?

The question of whether military spending should be decreased to allocate more funds for social welfare programs is a complex issue that has been debated for decades. Those who support this idea argue that the military budget is excessive and that funds should be redirected to support social welfare programs, such as education, healthcare, and housing. On the other hand, opponents argue that military spending is necessary to ensure national security and protect against potential threats.

One argument in favour of decreasing military spending is that it would free up resources to address pressing social issues, such as poverty, inequality, and unemployment. Social welfare programs could help to provide vital support for vulnerable populations, including children, the elderly, and those with disabilities, and could help to promote social justice and equality. Another argument is that excessive military spending can contribute to a cycle of violence and conflict, which may have far-reaching consequences for both domestic and international security. By redirecting resources away from military programs, governments could help to reduce tensions and promote peace and stability.

However, opponents argue that military spending is necessary to ensure national security and protect against potential threats, both domestic and international. They argue that cutting military spending could weaken the country's defence capabilities, leaving it vulnerable to attack and undermining its standing in the international community.

In conclusion, the question of whether military spending should be decreased to allocate more funds for social welfare programs is a complex issue that requires careful consideration and analysis. While there are strong arguments on both sides, policymakers must carefully balance national security concerns with the need to address pressing social issues and promote social justice and equality.

119. To what extent should autonomous weapons be allowed in military operations?

The question of whether autonomous weapons should be allowed in military operations is a highly complex issue. Autonomous weapons, also known as lethal autonomous weapons systems (LAWS), are weapons that can operate without human intervention, using artificial intelligence to identify and engage targets.

Those who support the use of autonomous weapons argue that they can improve military efficiency and reduce the risk of human casualties. They also argue that autonomous weapons could be used to carry out complex missions that would be too dangerous or difficult for human soldiers. However, opponents argue that the use of autonomous weapons poses significant ethical, legal, and practical challenges. They argue that the use of autonomous weapons could result in unintended consequences, such as civilian casualties or the loss of control over the weapon. They also argue that the use of autonomous weapons raises fundamental questions about the morality of delegating life and death decisions to machines.

To address these concerns, some experts have proposed guidelines and regulations for the use of autonomous weapons, including requirements for human oversight and accountability. Others have called for a complete ban on the development and use of autonomous weapons, arguing that they pose a threat to human security and dignity.

In conclusion, the question of whether autonomous weapons should be allowed in military operations is a complex and contentious issue that requires careful consideration and analysis. While there may be benefits to the use of autonomous weapons, policymakers must carefully weigh these benefits against the ethical, legal, and practical challenges posed by these weapons. Ultimately, any decision on the use of autonomous weapons must prioritise human security and dignity, while also taking into account the evolving nature of warfare and technology.

120. Should countries to be allowed to acquire and maintain their own nuclear arsenals?

The question of whether countries should be allowed to acquire and maintain their own nuclear arsenals is a highly debated issue. Proponents of nuclear weapons argue that they are necessary to deter aggression and maintain international security, while opponents argue that the use of nuclear weapons would result in catastrophic consequences that would far outweigh any potential benefits.

One of the main arguments in favour of allowing countries to acquire and maintain their own nuclear arsenals is the principle of national sovereignty. Many countries view nuclear weapons as a symbol of national power and prestige, and argue that they have the right to acquire and maintain these weapons for their own defence.

However, opponents argue that the use of nuclear weapons would violate the principles of just war theory, which requires that military force be used only as a last resort, and that the harm caused by the use of force must be proportionate to the goal being pursued. Given the immense harm that would be caused by the use of nuclear weapons, it is difficult to argue that their use would ever be proportionate to any legitimate military objective. Furthermore, the acquisition and maintenance of nuclear arsenals can contribute to a cycle of arms escalation and competition, which can increase the risk of accidental or intentional nuclear war.

In conclusion, the question of whether countries should be allowed to acquire and maintain their own nuclear arsenals is a complex and contentious issue that requires careful consideration and analysis. While some may argue that national sovereignty justifies the acquisition and maintenance of nuclear weapons, the overwhelming consensus among policymakers and scholars is that the use of nuclear weapons would be unjustifiable and morally reprehensible under any circumstance. Governments should instead prioritise international cooperation, disarmament, and non-proliferation efforts to reduce the risk of nuclear war and promote global security.

121. Should there be limits on the use of drone strikes in counter-terrorism operations?

The question of whether there should be limits on the use of drone strikes in counter-terrorism operations is a highly debated issue. Drone strikes, also known as targeted killings, are a form of military operation in which unmanned aerial vehicles (UAVs) are used to launch missiles at suspected terrorists.

Proponents of drone strikes argue that they are a precise and effective tool in the fight against terrorism, and that they can help to avoid civilian casualties and limit collateral damage. They also argue that drone strikes can be used to target high-value terrorists who are difficult to capture or kill through other means.

However, opponents argue that drone strikes pose significant ethical, legal, and practical challenges. They argue that drone strikes violate international law and human rights, and that they can lead to the deaths of innocent civilians and the radicalisation of local populations. They also argue that the use of drone strikes can undermine the rule of law and due process, as suspects are targeted without trial or conviction. To address these concerns, some experts have proposed guidelines and regulations for the use of drone strikes, including requirements for transparency, accountability, and oversight. Others have called for a complete ban on the use of drone strikes, arguing that they pose a threat to international security and human rights.

In conclusion, the question of whether there should be limits on the use of drone strikes in counter-terrorism operations is a complex and contentious issue that requires careful consideration and analysis. While there may be benefits to the use of drone strikes, policymakers must carefully weigh these benefits against the ethical, legal, and practical challenges posed by these strikes. Ultimately, any decision on the use of drone strikes must prioritise human security and dignity, while also taking into account the evolving nature of warfare and technology.

122. Is it appropriate for military organisations to collaborate with private intelligence firms?

The question of whether it is appropriate for military organisations to collaborate with private intelligence firms is a complex issue that raises significant ethical, legal, and practical concerns. Private intelligence firms, also known as private military and security companies (PMSCs), are private companies that provide intelligence, security, and other services to governments, military organisations, and other clients.

Proponents of collaboration with private intelligence firms argue that these firms can provide specialised expertise and capabilities that are not available within military organisations, and that they can help to fill gaps in intelligence and security capabilities. They also argue that collaboration with private intelligence firms can help to reduce the cost and administrative burden of intelligence gathering and analysis.

However, opponents argue that collaboration with private intelligence firms can undermine the rule of law and democratic accountability, as these firms may not be subject to the same legal and regulatory frameworks as government agencies. They also argue that private intelligence firms may prioritise profit over public interest, and that their methods and practices may be unethical or illegal. To address these concerns, some experts have proposed guidelines and regulations for the use of private intelligence firms, including requirements for transparency, accountability, and oversight. Others have called for a complete ban on the use of private intelligence firms, arguing that these firms pose a threat to national security and democratic values.

In conclusion, the question of whether it is appropriate for military organisations to collaborate with private intelligence firms is a complex and contentious issue that requires careful consideration and analysis. While there may be benefits to collaboration with private intelligence firms, policymakers must carefully weigh these benefits against the ethical, legal, and practical challenges posed by such collaboration. Ultimately, any decision on collaboration with private intelligence firms must prioritise national security and democratic values, while also taking into account the evolving nature of intelligence gathering and analysis.

123. Should private companies be allowed to develop and sell military weapons and technology?

The question of whether private companies should be allowed to develop and sell military weapons and technology is a contentious and complex issue that raises significant ethical, legal, and practical concerns. Private companies, particularly those in the defence industry, have long played a significant role in the development and production of military weapons and technology.

Proponents of allowing private companies to develop and sell military weapons and technology argue that these companies can provide innovative and cost-effective solutions to military needs. They also argue that competition in the defence industry can lead to improved quality, efficiency, and responsiveness to military requirements. However, opponents argue that allowing private companies to develop and sell military weapons and technology can have negative consequences. They argue that private companies may prioritise profit over public interest and national security, and that the use of private companies can lead to conflicts of interest, lack of transparency, and inadequate oversight. They also argue that the use of private companies can undermine democratic accountability, as these companies may not be subject to the same legal and regulatory frameworks as government agencies.

To address these concerns, some experts have proposed guidelines and regulations for the use of private companies in the development and production of military weapons and technology. These guidelines and regulations may include requirements for transparency, accountability, and oversight, as well as restrictions on the types of weapons and technology that private companies can develop and sell.

In conclusion, the question of whether private companies should be allowed to develop and sell military weapons and technology is a complex and contested issue that requires careful consideration and analysis. While there may be benefits to the use of private companies in the defence industry, policymakers must carefully weigh these benefits against the ethical, legal, and practical challenges posed by the use of private companies. Ultimately, any decision on the use of private companies must prioritise national security and public interest, while also taking into account the evolving nature of warfare and technology.

124. Should the use of chemical and biological weapons be considered a red line in international conflicts?

The use of chemical and biological weapons is considered to be a serious violation of international law and humanitarian norms. Chemical and biological weapons are designed to cause widespread and indiscriminate harm, and their use can have devastating effects on civilian populations and the environment.

Therefore, many countries and international organisations consider the use of chemical and biological weapons to be a red line in international conflicts. This means that the use of these weapons is considered to be a significant violation of international law and may trigger a strong international response, including military intervention or sanctions. One of the key reasons for this red line is the potential for chemical and biological weapons to cause widespread and indiscriminate harm. These weapons can be difficult to control and may affect not only military targets but also civilian populations and the environment. The use of these weapons can also create long-lasting and far-reaching health and environmental consequences.

Another reason for this red line is the potential for chemical and biological weapons to be used by non-state actors, such as terrorist organisations or rogue states. The use of these weapons by non-state actors can be particularly difficult to deter or respond to, and may pose a significant threat to global security.

In conclusion, the use of chemical and biological weapons is considered to be a red line in international conflicts due to their potential for indiscriminate harm and long-lasting consequences. The use of these weapons is a serious violation of international law and humanitarian norms, and may trigger a strong international response. It is important for the international community to work together to prevent the proliferation and use of these weapons, and to hold accountable those who violate this red line.

125. Is pre-emptive military action ever justified to prevent the proliferation of weapons of mass destruction?

Pre-emptive military action is a complex issue, particularly when it comes to the prevention of the proliferation of weapons of mass destruction (WMDs). Pre-emptive military action involves attacking an adversary before they are able to attack, in order to prevent an imminent threat.

While the prevention of the proliferation of WMDs is an important goal, pre-emptive military action to achieve this goal raises significant ethical, legal, and practical concerns. First, it can be difficult to determine with certainty that an adversary is developing WMDs and intends to use them. Second, pre-emptive military action can have significant human and economic costs, including loss of life, destruction of infrastructure, and long-lasting regional instability. Third, pre-emptive military action can undermine international law and norms, including the UN Charter, which prohibits the use of force except in self-defence or with the authorisation of the UN Security Council.

While there may be situations where pre-emptive military action is necessary to prevent the proliferation of WMDs, any decision to use pre-emptive military action must be guided by a careful consideration of the ethical, legal, and practical concerns. It must also take into account the potential long-term consequences of such actions and the impact on regional stability and global security. In many cases, diplomatic and non-military approaches may be more effective in preventing the proliferation of WMDs, and should be prioritised wherever possible.

126. Is it ethical for governments to use propaganda and psychological operations in warfare?

The use of propaganda and psychological operations in warfare raises complex ethical questions. Propaganda refers to the dissemination of information, often with a biased or misleading slant, in order to influence public opinion or behaviour. Psychological operations (PSYOP) involve the use of information and communication techniques to influence the attitudes and behaviour of an adversary.

On the one hand, some argue that propaganda and PSYOP are legitimate tools of warfare, particularly in situations where military action is necessary to protect national security or the lives of citizens. These tools can be used to demoralise enemy forces, create confusion and mistrust, and deter aggression. In some cases, propaganda and PSYOP can be used to avoid the need for more violent or destructive military action.

On the other hand, others argue that the use of propaganda and PSYOP is unethical and undermines democratic values. These tools can be used to spread false information, manipulate public opinion, and violate the principles of free speech and transparency. The use of propaganda and PSYOP can also create long-lasting social and psychological effects, particularly when used against civilian populations.

In conclusion, the use of propaganda and psychological operations in warfare raises complex ethical questions. While these tools may be used to achieve military objectives, they can also undermine democratic values and have long-lasting social and psychological effects. Any decision to use propaganda and PSYOP must be guided by a careful consideration of the ethical implications and the potential impact on civilian populations.

127. Is it necessary to prioritise non-military approaches, such as economic aid and diplomacy, over military solutions to resolve conflicts?

Yes, there should be a greater focus on non-military solutions to conflicts, such as diplomacy and economic aid. Military interventions can have devastating consequences, including loss of life, displacement, and long-term social and economic damage. Diplomacy and economic aid, on the other hand, can help to prevent conflicts from escalating and promote long-term stability.

Diplomacy involves the use of negotiation and dialogue to resolve disputes and find common ground. By engaging in dialogue with adversaries, it may be possible to identify shared interests and find peaceful solutions to conflicts. Economic aid can help to support vulnerable communities and promote economic development, which can in turn reduce the likelihood of conflict. Providing economic assistance to countries can help to address root causes of conflict, such as poverty and inequality.

In addition, non-military solutions can help to build trust and foster long-term relationships between countries. Diplomacy and economic aid can create opportunities for collaboration and cooperation, which can lead to greater stability and prosperity. This can ultimately reduce the need for military intervention and promote a more peaceful world. In conclusion, there should be a greater focus on non-military solutions to conflicts, such as diplomacy and economic aid. By prioritising these approaches, we can promote long-term stability, reduce the likelihood of conflict, and create a more peaceful world.

128. Should countries be held accountable for the use of military force against non-state actors operating within their borders?

The question of whether countries should be held accountable for the use of military force against non-state actors operating within their borders is a complex one. On the one hand, countries have a responsibility to protect their citizens from violent extremist groups and other non-state actors who threaten their security. In some cases, military force may be necessary to achieve this objective.

On the other hand, the use of military force against non-state actors can have significant humanitarian consequences, including civilian casualties, displacement, and the erosion of human rights. Additionally, military interventions can have unintended consequences, including the strengthening of extremist groups and the perpetuation of conflict.

Therefore, it is important to ensure that countries are held accountable for their actions and that military force is only used as a last resort. This can be achieved through international law and institutions, such as the International Criminal Court and the United Nations Security Council. These bodies can investigate and prosecute individuals and countries that engage in illegal military interventions or human rights violations.

In addition, it is important to explore non-military solutions to address the underlying drivers of conflict and extremism, such as poverty, inequality, and political exclusion. By addressing these root causes, it may be possible to reduce the need for military intervention and promote long-term stability. In conclusion, while countries have a responsibility to protect their citizens from non-state actors, the use of military force must be carefully considered and only used as a last resort. Countries should be held accountable for their actions, and efforts should be made to explore non-military solutions to address the underlying drivers of conflict and extremism.

129. Should the military be involved in domestic law enforcement and border security?

The involvement of the military in domestic law enforcement and border security is a contentious issue. While some argue that military support can enhance border security and law enforcement capabilities, others argue that it can result in the militarisation of law enforcement and the erosion of civil liberties.

There are several potential benefits to involving the military in domestic law enforcement and border security. Military personnel are trained in specialised skills, such as surveillance and intelligence gathering, that can be useful in detecting and preventing criminal activity. In addition, military resources, such as equipment and personnel, can be deployed quickly to respond to emergencies or other security threats.

However, there are also significant risks associated with military involvement in domestic law enforcement and border security. The use of military force can create a culture of aggression and violence, which can result in human rights violations and the erosion of civil liberties. Additionally, military personnel may not be trained in the nuances of domestic law enforcement and may not have the same legal and ethical constraints as civilian law enforcement.

Therefore, it is important to approach military involvement in domestic law enforcement and border security with caution. Any such involvement should be carefully regulated and monitored to ensure that civil liberties are protected and that military personnel are held accountable for any violations. In addition, efforts should be made to strengthen civilian law enforcement and border security capabilities to reduce the need for military involvement. In conclusion, while there may be benefits to involving the military in domestic law enforcement and border security, such involvement must be approached with caution. It is important to carefully regulate and monitor military involvement to protect civil liberties and ensure accountability, while also strengthening civilian law enforcement and border security capabilities.

130. Can the use of torture be justified in the interrogation of suspected terrorists?

The use of torture in the interrogation of suspected terrorists is a divisive issue. While some argue that torture may be necessary to extract critical information that could save lives and prevent terrorist attacks, others argue that torture is inhumane and violates basic human rights.

In addition, there is evidence to suggest that torture is not an effective means of extracting reliable information. Suspects may be more likely to provide false information or withhold information when subjected to torture, as they may provide whatever information they think will make the torture stop. Furthermore, the use of torture undermines the moral authority of those who use it and can be used as propaganda by terrorist groups to justify their own acts of violence. As a result, many international human rights organisations, including the United Nations, have condemned the use of torture as a violation of human rights and international law.

While the need to prevent terrorism is a legitimate concern, the use of torture is not an acceptable means of achieving this objective. Rather, alternative approaches, such as rapport-building techniques, should be used to build trust and establish a rapport with suspects, with a focus on gathering intelligence through non-coercive means.

In conclusion, while the use of torture in the interrogation of suspected terrorists may seem justified in some cases, it is not an acceptable or effective means of gathering reliable intelligence. Instead, non-coercive approaches should be used to build trust and establish rapport with suspects to gather critical information.

131. Should countries have a moral duty to intervene in cases of genocide and mass atrocities, even if it requires violating national sovereignty?

The issue of whether countries have a moral duty to intervene in cases of genocide and mass atrocities, even if it means violating national sovereignty, is a complex and contentious one. On one hand, it can be argued that there is a moral obligation to protect innocent civilians from atrocities and prevent further human suffering. In cases where a government is unable or unwilling to protect its own citizens from such atrocities, external intervention may be necessary to prevent the continuation of such crimes.

On the other hand, the concept of national sovereignty is an important principle of international relations, and the violation of a country's sovereignty can have serious implications for international stability and security. There are also concerns that external interventions may exacerbate conflicts or result in unintended consequences, such as further violence or instability.

Despite these challenges, the international community has established several legal frameworks, such as the Responsibility to Protect (R2P) doctrine, that affirm the moral duty of countries to intervene in cases of genocide and mass atrocities. However, the decision to intervene should be based on careful consideration of the situation on the ground, the feasibility of intervention, and the potential consequences of such action.

In conclusion, while the principle of national sovereignty is important, the moral obligation to protect innocent civilians from genocide and mass atrocities cannot be ignored. Any decision to intervene must be carefully weighed, taking into account the potential consequences and the feasibility of action.

132. Should there be a global ban on the use of landmines and cluster munitions in warfare?

Yes, there should be a global ban on the use of landmines and cluster munitions in warfare. These weapons are indiscriminate and pose a significant threat to civilians long after a conflict has ended. Landmines, in particular, have been responsible for the deaths and injuries of countless innocent people, including children and farmers, who come into contact with them long after they have been planted.

Cluster munitions, on the other hand, release many small bomblets over a wide area, often failing to detonate on impact and thus becoming de facto landmines. These unexploded ordnances can remain a danger for years after a conflict has ended, killing and maiming innocent people who inadvertently come into contact with them.

The use of these weapons violates international humanitarian law, which seeks to protect civilians and limit the suffering caused by armed conflicts. The Convention on Certain Conventional Weapons (CCW) and the Convention on Cluster Munitions (CCM) are international agreements that ban or restrict the use of these weapons.

However, not all countries have signed or ratified these agreements, and the continued use of landmines and cluster munitions in conflicts around the world is a clear indication of the need for a global ban. Such a ban would send a clear message that the international community is committed to protecting civilians and preventing unnecessary suffering in armed conflicts.

133. Should countries be allowed to engage in cyber espionage and sabotage against their economic rivals?

No, countries should not be allowed to engage in cyber espionage and sabotage against their economic rivals. Such actions violate international laws and norms and can have serious negative consequences for the targeted country and its citizens.

Cyber espionage and sabotage can involve stealing confidential information, disrupting critical infrastructure, and manipulating data and systems to cause economic harm or gain a competitive advantage. These activities can have significant economic, social, and political repercussions and can potentially escalate into full-blown cyber warfare. Moreover, cyber espionage and sabotage are difficult to detect and attribute, which can lead to misunderstandings, mistrust, and even conflict between nations. The use of these tactics undermines the principles of international law and diplomacy, as well as the norms of good governance and fair competition.

Instead of engaging in cyber espionage and sabotage, countries should focus on developing and implementing strong cybersecurity measures to protect their own systems and critical infrastructure. Diplomatic channels and legal mechanisms should also be used to address disputes and grievances related to economic competition and intellectual property rights. Ultimately, cooperation and dialogue are key to fostering trust, stability, and prosperity in the global economy.

134. How can the military balance the need for operational security with the need for transparency and accountability to the public?

The military can balance the need for operational security with transparency and accountability to the public by implementing appropriate policies and practices. Some potential strategies include:

1. <u>Developing clear guidelines for information sharing</u>: The military can establish clear protocols for sharing information with the public and other stakeholders. These guidelines should take into account the need for operational security and the potential risks of releasing sensitive information, while also prioritising transparency and accountability.

2. <u>Providing regular updates</u>: The military can provide regular updates on its activities and operations through official channels such as press releases, social media, and public briefings. These updates can help to build trust and confidence in the military's activities while also providing the public with valuable information about national security issues.

3. <u>Conducting internal reviews</u>: The military can conduct regular internal reviews of its activities and operations to ensure that they are being conducted in accordance with established policies and guidelines. These reviews can also identify areas where improvements can be made to enhance transparency and accountability.

4. <u>Engaging with the public</u>: The military can engage with the public through outreach activities such as town hall meetings, public forums, and social media interactions. These activities can help to build trust and foster a sense of shared responsibility between the military and the public.

5. <u>Enforcing accountability</u>: The military can enforce accountability through mechanisms such as internal investigations, disciplinary actions, and external oversight. These measures can help to ensure that the military is held accountable for its actions and that appropriate action is taken in cases of misconduct or wrongdoing.

By implementing these strategies, the military can balance the need for operational security with transparency and accountability to the public, thereby promoting trust and confidence in its activities and operations.

135. What role does leadership play in shaping the success or failure of military campaigns and operations?

Leadership plays a critical role in shaping the success or failure of military campaigns and operations. Effective leaders are able to inspire and motivate their troops, develop and execute clear strategies, and adapt to changing circumstances on the battlefield. In contrast, poor leadership can result in confusion, disorganisation, and morale problems that can undermine the effectiveness of military operations.

One key aspect of effective military leadership is the ability to develop and communicate a clear vision and strategy. This involves setting goals, identifying priorities, and outlining a plan for achieving success. Leaders must also be able to communicate this vision to their troops and ensure that everyone is working towards a common goal. Another important aspect of effective military leadership is the ability to adapt to changing circumstances on the battlefield. This involves being able to recognise and respond to new challenges, adjust plans and tactics as necessary, and remain flexible in the face of uncertainty and complexity.

Effective military leaders must also be able to inspire and motivate their troops. This involves fostering a sense of camaraderie and teamwork, recognising and rewarding good performance, and leading by example. Leaders must also be able to maintain morale and motivation in the face of adversity and hardship.

In summary, leadership plays a critical role in shaping the success or failure of military campaigns and operations. Effective leaders are able to develop and communicate a clear vision and strategy, adapt to changing circumstances on the battlefield, and inspire and motivate their troops to achieve success.

136. What are the challenges faced by the military in implementing its doctrines and strategies in modern warfare scenarios?

The modern battlefield is characterised by rapid technological advances and evolving threats, presenting a range of challenges for military forces in implementing their doctrines and strategies.

One of the key challenges faced by the military is the need to adapt to new forms of warfare, including cyber attacks, unconventional warfare, and terrorism. These threats often require different tactics and strategies than traditional forms of warfare, and may require specialised training and equipment for troops.

Another challenge is the need to balance the use of technology with the need for human decision-making and judgment. While advances in technology can provide new capabilities and advantages on the battlefield, they can also lead to an over-reliance on technology and automation, which can have negative consequences in complex and unpredictable environments.

The increasing interconnectedness and complexity of the modern battlefield also presents challenges for military forces in terms of coordination and communication. Military operations may involve multiple agencies, organisations, and partners, requiring effective communication and coordination to ensure that everyone is working towards a common goal. Finally, the need to operate within the constraints of international law and public opinion presents challenges for military forces in implementing their doctrines and strategies. Military forces must balance the need for security and effectiveness with the need to respect human rights and the rule of law, and must also be able to justify their actions to the public and international community.

In summary, the challenges faced by the military in implementing its doctrines and strategies in modern warfare scenarios include the need to adapt to new forms of warfare, balance the use of technology with human decision-making, coordinate with multiple partners, and operate within legal and ethical constraints.

137. How can military alliances and partnerships effectively address global security challenges, particularly in the context of shifting geopolitical dynamics?

Military alliances and partnerships are essential for addressing global security challenges, particularly in the context of shifting geopolitical dynamics. To effectively address these challenges, military alliances and partnerships should focus on the following areas:

1. <u>Strengthening interoperability and coordination</u>: Military forces from different countries should be able to work together effectively in joint operations. This requires regular training and exercise to build trust and ensure that forces are able to communicate and coordinate effectively.
2. <u>Developing shared strategies and doctrines</u>: Military alliances and partnerships should work to develop shared strategies and doctrines to address common threats. This can help to ensure that forces are working towards common goals and can share resources and intelligence.
3. <u>Encouraging burdern-sharing and resource pooling</u>: Military alliances and partnerships should encourage member countries to share the burden of providing security, including through contributions of troops, resources, and expertise. This can help to ensure that no one country bears the full cost of maintaining security.
4. <u>Adapting to changing threats and geopolitical dynamics</u>: Military alliances and partnerships should be flexible and adaptable, able to respond quickly to changing threats and shifting geopolitical dynamics. This requires regular assessments of threats and capabilities, as well as a willingness to adjust strategies and tactics as necessary.
5. <u>Maintaining open communication and transparency</u>: Military alliances and partnerships should maintain open communication and transparency with each other, as well as with the public and international community. This can help to build trust and confidence, and ensure that actions are seen as legitimate and justified.

Overall, effective military alliances and partnerships require a commitment to shared goals, open communication, and a willingness to adapt and evolve in response to changing threats and geopolitical dynamics.

138. What are the ethical implications of using military force and how can they be effectively addressed in decision-making processes?

Using military force in any situation carries significant ethical implications, and it is critical to address these implications during the decision-making process. The decision to use military force can result in the loss of life and can have far-reaching consequences for the individuals involved and their families, as well as for the broader community and international relations.

One approach to addressing the ethical implications of using military force is to adopt a just war theory, which provides a framework for evaluating the ethical considerations involved in the decision to go to war and in the conduct of war. This theory requires that military action meets certain criteria, such as a just cause, proportionality, and discrimination, and it can help guide decision-making by providing a systematic way to evaluate the ethical implications of military force.

Another approach is to ensure that decision-making processes are transparent, inclusive, and informed by diverse perspectives. Leaders must consider the perspectives of stakeholders, including the military, government, and civil society, and engage in open and honest dialogue about the ethical implications of military force. This can help ensure that the decision to use military force is well-informed and that the ethical implications of military action are carefully considered.

Finally, ongoing training and education for military personnel can help ensure that ethical considerations are central to military operations. Military personnel must be equipped with the knowledge and skills necessary to make ethical decisions in complex and rapidly changing situations, and ongoing training can help ensure that these skills are maintained and reinforced. By addressing the ethical implications of military force through these approaches, decision-makers can ensure that the use of military force is consistent with ethical principles and serves the broader interests of society.

139. How can the military effectively engage with local communities and stakeholders in conflict-affected regions, and what role can civil-military relations play in achieving

long-term stability and peace?

Effective engagement with local communities and stakeholders in conflict-affected regions is a crucial component of military operations, particularly in achieving long-term stability and peace. To achieve this, the military must be sensitive to the cultural and social norms of the communities they are interacting with, and must prioritise building trust and cooperation through open and transparent communication.

Civil-military relations can play a key role in achieving these objectives. By establishing positive relationships with local civil society organisations, NGOs, and other stakeholders, the military can leverage their expertise and resources to gain a better understanding of the needs and priorities of the communities they are working with. This can help to foster greater trust and cooperation between military and civilian actors, and ensure that military interventions are sensitive to local contexts and responsive to local needs.

To effectively engage with local communities, the military should prioritise communication and outreach, through public events, town hall meetings, and other forums that allow for open and transparent dialogue. The military should also prioritise the recruitment and training of local personnel, who can serve as key cultural liaisons between military forces and local communities.

Finally, the military must prioritise the protection of civilians and respect for human rights, both in their interactions with local communities and in their conduct of military operations. By adhering to these ethical principles, the military can help to build trust and cooperation with local stakeholders, and contribute to the achievement of long-term stability and peace in conflict-affected regions.

140. What is the future of nuclear deterrence and disarmament, particularly in the context of increasing proliferation risks and the emergence of new nuclear powers?

The future of nuclear deterrence and disarmament is a topic of significant concern in the international community. While many countries advocate for complete disarmament, others argue that nuclear weapons are necessary for deterrence and national security.

One of the main challenges in achieving nuclear disarmament is the increasing proliferation of nuclear weapons, which poses a significant risk to global security. The emergence of new nuclear powers, such as North Korea, has further complicated efforts to reduce nuclear arsenals. Additionally, there is a concern that terrorist groups may acquire nuclear weapons, which would have catastrophic consequences.

To address these challenges, it is essential for the international community to work together to prevent the spread of nuclear weapons and to strengthen existing nonproliferation agreements. Additionally, efforts should be made to reduce the role of nuclear weapons in military strategies, which would contribute to decreasing the risks of nuclear use. Furthermore, nuclear-armed states should work towards reducing their nuclear arsenals and eventually complete disarmament. However, this is a complex process that requires careful planning and negotiation. Confidence-building measures, transparency, and verification mechanisms are essential to building trust and ensuring compliance.

In conclusion, the future of nuclear deterrence and disarmament is dependent on the commitment of the international community to address proliferation risks, reduce the role of nuclear weapons in military strategies, and work towards disarmament through negotiation and cooperation.

141. Should countries pursue territorial expansion in pursuit of national security?

Territorial expansion is often pursued in the name of national security, but it can also lead to conflicts and instability. The pursuit of territorial expansion can violate the sovereignty of other nations and result in tensions and conflicts, as seen in the annexation of Crimea by Russia and the territorial disputes in the South China Sea.

Countries should prioritise diplomacy and peaceful means of resolving conflicts, rather than resorting to military force or territorial expansion. The use of force and expansionism can result in long-term consequences, such as resentment and hostility from neighbouring nations and international condemnation.

Instead, countries can focus on building strong relationships with their neighbours, fostering economic cooperation and development, and investing in their own national defence capabilities to ensure their security. A cooperative and collaborative approach to security can lead to more stable and peaceful regions and promote global security.

142. *To what extent should civilians be involved in military decision-making processes?*

Civilians can play a crucial role in shaping military decision-making processes. Their perspectives can provide valuable insights into the wider social and political consequences of military actions. However, there are limits to the extent to which civilians should be involved in these processes, as military decisions must ultimately be made by those with the necessary expertise and training.

One way in which civilians can be involved in military decision-making is through democratic oversight of military activities. Elected officials, such as members of parliament or congress, can hold the military accountable to the public and ensure that military decisions are consistent with broader political goals. Another way in which civilians can contribute to military decision-making is through participation in advisory committees or consultative bodies. These bodies can provide diverse perspectives and ensure that the military takes into account a range of perspectives when making decisions.

However, there are risks associated with involving civilians in military decision-making. Civilians may lack the necessary technical expertise or may be influenced by political or ideological considerations. This could lead to decisions that are not in the best interests of national security or that undermine military effectiveness.

Therefore, the extent to which civilians should be involved in military decision-making should be carefully considered, taking into account the specific context and the potential risks and benefits of civilian participation.

143. *What is the role of gender in military operations and how can it be better integrated into military planning?*

The role of gender in military operations is multifaceted and complex. Historically, military operations have been male-dominated, with women excluded from combat roles or relegated to supporting roles. However, in recent years, there has been a growing recognition of the importance of gender perspectives in military planning, particularly in conflict zones where women and children are often the most vulnerable.

The integration of gender perspectives into military planning involves understanding the different roles and experiences of men and women in conflict, and the ways in which gender norms and power dynamics can exacerbate conflict or contribute to peace-building efforts. This requires not only the inclusion of women in military decision-making processes but also a broader effort to ensure that women's perspectives and experiences are heard and valued in all aspects of military planning.

Furthermore, the military has a responsibility to address issues of gender-based violence within its own ranks and in conflict zones. This includes providing training on gender-sensitive approaches to military operations, ensuring that sexual exploitation and abuse are not tolerated, and addressing the needs and rights of women and children in post-conflict situations. In conclusion, the role of gender in military operations is crucial, and there is a need for better integration of gender perspectives into military planning. This can help to promote greater understanding of the impact of conflict on different groups, and contribute to more effective and sustainable peace-building efforts.

144. How can militaries better incorporate emerging technologies, such as artificial intelligence and quantum computing, into their operations?

The integration of emerging technologies into military operations has the potential to transform the way militaries operate, increasing their efficiency, speed, and effectiveness. Artificial intelligence (AI) and quantum computing, in particular, offer significant advantages for military applications, such as autonomous weapons systems, predictive maintenance of equipment, and decision-making support systems.

To better incorporate these technologies, militaries should invest in research and development programs, collaborate with technology companies and academic institutions, and train personnel in the use of new technologies. Additionally, it is essential to establish ethical and legal frameworks for the development and use of these technologies to ensure their responsible implementation.

Moreover, militaries should prioritise cybersecurity to protect against potential cyber threats to emerging technologies. This will require investments in cybersecurity training, development of secure communication channels and protocols, and the adoption of best practices for cybersecurity. Furthermore, the integration of emerging technologies in military operations should also involve an assessment of the potential impact on human resources, including potential job displacement, retraining needs, and workforce diversity.

Overall, the incorporation of emerging technologies into military operations can enhance military capabilities and effectiveness, but it requires careful planning and investment, as well as the establishment of ethical and legal frameworks to ensure responsible use.

145. How can militaries balance the need for secrecy and security with the public's right to information and transparency?

Balancing the need for secrecy and security with the public's right to information and transparency is a delicate task that militaries face. On the one hand, it is essential to maintain operational security and protect classified information to prevent adversaries from gaining an advantage. On the other hand, transparency and accountability are necessary for maintaining public trust and ensuring that the military is acting in the best interests of the nation.

One approach is to establish clear policies and procedures for classifying and declassifying information. This includes defining what types of information should be classified and for how long, as well as establishing clear criteria for declassifying information. This will enable the public to better understand what information can and cannot be shared, and provide greater transparency around decision-making processes. Additionally, militaries can leverage technology to enhance transparency and public access to information while still protecting sensitive information. For example, digital platforms can be used to share information about military operations and activities in real-time, while also enabling military personnel to communicate securely and confidentially.

Finally, it is essential to build and maintain trust with the public through engagement and communication. This can involve engaging with media, civil society groups, and other stakeholders to share information and provide context for military actions. By doing so, militaries can help the public better understand their role in national security and build support for their actions.

146. Is the current global arms trade ethical, and what measures can be taken to regulate it more effectively?

The global arms trade raises significant ethical concerns, particularly concerning the impact of the trade on conflict and human rights. The sale and transfer of weapons can fuel conflicts, perpetuate human rights abuses, and destabilise regions. Additionally, the lack of transparency and accountability in the arms trade can contribute to corruption and illicit trafficking.

To regulate the arms trade more effectively, several measures can be taken. Firstly, increased transparency and accountability are essential. This includes more rigorous reporting requirements for arms transfers, as well as stricter controls on end-users and end-uses. The United Nations Arms Trade Treaty, which aims to regulate the international trade in conventional weapons, is a step in this direction.

Secondly, stronger regulations on the sale and transfer of weapons should be implemented. This includes ensuring that countries only sell arms to governments that have demonstrated a commitment to respecting human rights and international humanitarian law. Additionally, stricter controls on the sale and transfer of weapons to conflict zones should be implemented. Finally, there should be greater international cooperation in addressing the arms trade. This includes sharing information and intelligence on illicit trafficking and promoting greater coordination between law enforcement agencies. Ultimately, a more ethical global arms trade requires a concerted effort by governments, international organisations, and civil society to regulate and monitor the trade in weapons.

147. Is there a need for a global ban on the development and use of killer robots, and what are the potential implications of their use in warfare?

Killer robots, also known as autonomous weapons systems, are a rapidly developing area of military technology. These are weapons that can select and engage targets without human intervention. Many experts believe that their development and use pose significant ethical and legal challenges, particularly as they could potentially be used to target civilians or cause unintended harm.

There is growing concern about the potential risks of killer robots and the need for regulation to ensure their responsible development and use. Some argue that a global ban on these weapons is necessary to prevent a dangerous arms race and the proliferation of such technologies. The use of killer robots in warfare also raises questions about accountability and responsibility for the actions of autonomous systems. As these systems make decisions independently, it is unclear who should be held responsible for any harm caused by their actions.

To address these challenges, many experts have called for the development of international norms and standards for the development and use of autonomous weapons systems. These could include requirements for human oversight and accountability, as well as limitations on the use of such weapons. It is important to consider the implications of these weapons and to engage in a broader discussion about the role of autonomy in warfare. The development and use of killer robots raise significant ethical and legal questions that must be carefully considered to ensure that military technology is developed and used in a responsible and ethical manner.

148. Is the practice of targeted killings morally justifiable in the context of counterterrorism?

The practice of targeted killings, or the intentional killing of specific individuals believed to pose a threat to national security, is a highly debated issue with significant moral implications. While some argue that targeted killings are necessary for protecting national security and preventing terrorist attacks, others argue that they are morally unjustifiable and constitute extrajudicial killing.

Proponents of targeted killings argue that they are a necessary tool for counterterrorism, as they allow for the elimination of specific individuals who pose an imminent threat to national security. They argue that targeted killings are a more precise and effective alternative to conventional military operations, as they minimise the risk of collateral damage and civilian casualties.

Critics of targeted killings, however, argue that they violate the principles of due process and international law, as they involve the killing of individuals without trial or judicial oversight. They argue that the practice is morally unjustifiable and constitutes extrajudicial killing, and that it undermines the rule of law and human rights.

In conclusion, the moral justifiability of targeted killings remains a highly debated issue. While some argue that they are a necessary tool for protecting national security, others argue that they violate basic principles of due process and international law. It is important for policymakers to carefully consider the ethical implications of targeted killings and ensure that they are used only as a last resort, in accordance with international law and human rights standards.

149. Should soldiers be held accountable for war crimes committed during conflict, even if they were following orders?

Yes, soldiers should be held accountable for war crimes committed during conflict, even if they were following orders. The Nuremberg Trials after World War II established the principle that "superior orders" are not a defence for war crimes, and this principle has been reaffirmed in subsequent international law and conventions. Soldiers have a moral and legal obligation to refuse unlawful orders, and those who do carry out war crimes must be held accountable for their actions.

It is important to ensure that soldiers are trained and educated on international humanitarian law and the laws of armed conflict, so they can distinguish between lawful and unlawful orders. Additionally, military leaders have a responsibility to establish a culture of accountability and to enforce ethical conduct among their troops.

Holding soldiers accountable for war crimes sends a strong message that such actions will not be tolerated and can help to prevent future violations. It also helps to promote the rule of law and uphold human rights, which are essential for building peaceful and just societies.

150. How has India's defence modernisation programme evolved over the years, and what are the major priorities for the Indian Armed Forces in the coming years?

India's defence modernisation program has evolved significantly over the years, with a focus on indigenisation and self-sufficiency in defence production. The country's defence budget has increased steadily, with a focus on developing its air and naval capabilities, and enhancing its strategic reach.

In recent years, the Indian armed forces have focused on modernising their equipment and systems, with a particular emphasis on indigenously developed technologies. This has included the development of indigenous missile systems, fighter aircraft, and submarines, as well as the acquisition of modern equipment from other countries, such as the Rafale fighter jets from France.

In the coming years, the major priorities for the Indian armed forces are likely to include enhancing its defence capabilities along its borders with China and Pakistan, developing its cyber and space capabilities, and strengthening its naval and air defence capabilities. There is also likely to be a continued emphasis on indigenisation and self-reliance in defence production, with a view to reducing reliance on foreign suppliers and enhancing India's defence manufacturing base.

Overall, India's defence modernisation program reflects the country's growing strategic ambitions and its desire to assert itself as a major regional and global power. While there are still challenges to be addressed in terms of procurement and defence production, India's defence modernisation efforts are likely to continue to be a key priority in the coming years.

Disclaimer: While "The Definitive Guide to Defence and Strategic Studies: 150 Q&A for Mastery" has been written to provide accurate and up-to-date information, the author and publisher are not responsible for any errors or omissions or for any consequences arising from the use of the information contained in this book. The book is intended solely as a study aid and should not be used as a substitute for a complete course of study or professional advice. Readers should use their own judgment and consult with relevant experts as needed. The author and publisher do not guarantee the accuracy, completeness, or timeliness of the information presented in this book.

Afterword

As I reflect on the completion of this book, "The Definitive Guide to Defence and Strategic Studies: 150 Q&A for Mastery," I am filled with a sense of pride and accomplishment. This book is the culmination of years of hard-work, research, and dedication to the field of defence and strategic studies. I wrote this book with the aim of providing students enrolled in defence and strategic studies degree programmes with a comprehensive guide to the subject matter. I wanted to create a resource that would help students to master the subject matter and to deepen their understanding of this complex and important field.

I am pleased with the way the book has turned out. The questions and answers are designed to challenge the reader's knowledge and understanding, while providing a thorough explanation of the concepts and theories covered in each question. I hope that this book will serve as a valuable resource for students enrolled in defence and strategic studies degree, as well as anyone interested in the field. I also hope that it will inspire readers to continue their studies and to deepen their understanding of this important field.

In closing, I would like to thank everyone who has supported me throughout the writing of this book. I am grateful for the encouragement, feedback, and support that I received along the way. I hope this book will be a useful study aid and reference guide for many years to come.

Anirudh.R.Phadke

About The Editor

Anirudh.R.Phadke holds a Master of Science (Strategic Studies) and a certificate in Terrorism Studies from S. Rajaratnam School of International Studies (RSIS) at Nanyang Technological University (NTU). He completed Bachelor of Arts in Defence and Strategic Studies at Guru Nanak College. He is the Founder and Editor of The Viyug. He completed an (online) academic fellowship from The Heritage Foundation. He previosuly worked for an international law enforcement organisation based in Singapore. His research works has been published across various online news outlets based in India and abroad.

Books By The Editor

India-China Ladakh Standoff (2020)

From the period of the British Raj, the border issues between both the present Asian big powers existed. The Simla Convention put forth by Henry McMohan failed to formulate a definitive border between India, China, and Tibet. It ultimately leads to the Chinese annexation of Tibet. Thus from the year, 1950 the Chinese started executing massive Salami Slicing strategy to achieve their cartographic expansion goals. In the present-day scenario, the border has become a trump card for the Chinese to gain an upper hand against India whenever it tries to achieve an objective that has India's national interest merged in it. This paper analyses the current Ladakh Standoff including the Galwan Valley face off that occurred during the de-escalation process on 15th June 2020. Both the Indian and Chinese perspective are argued with proper facts and figures. As a bonus part satellites images of the Galwan Valley is discussed with proper explanation.

Research Papers On Defence And Strategic Studies Vol. 1: Strategy, India-China Affairs, And Cross-Strait Relations

Research Papers on Defence and Strategic Studies Vol. 1: Strategy, India-China Affairs, and Cross-Strait Relations is the finest collection of research papers, commentaries, and analyses on defence policy, military strategy, India-China diplomatic relations, and China - Taiwan issue.

Research Papers On Defence And Strategic Studies Vol. 2: Terrorism, Intelligence, And Cyber Warfare

Research Papers on Defence and Strategic Studies Vol. 2: Terrorism, Intelligence, and Cyber Warfare is the finest collection of research papers, commentaries, and analyses, on terrorism and counterterrorism studies, intelligence (espionage), religiously motivated terrorism, cyber warfare and many more.

About The Publisher

The Viyug (a Strategic and Defence Research Publication) is a leading source in producing finest of research papers, commentaries, analyses, books, podcasts, and other forms of media on various disciplines of international affairs such as geopolitics, defence and strategic studies, international relations, terrorism and counterterrorism studies, foreign and public policy, intelligence, political science, and similar fields. Our publications are well received and quoted by many international affairs' researchers and news outlets. The Viyug has a vast readership from various countries around the world and trusted by people from various walks of life. Our publications are available in all formats - digital, paperback, hardcover and printed across India, United Kingdom (UK), Canada, Japan, France, Australia, Poland, Sweden, Italy, Netherlands, Spain, Germany, and the United States of America (USA) for enabling global distribution. The Viyug also has established an education consulting wing to help students pursuing various disciplines/degrees from international affairs to find their career path.

THE END